*Collected
recollections
in honor of
Roe v. Wade*

Edited by
Elizabeth Lake
in collaboration with
NARAL Pro-Choice
Washington

IN OUR
OWN WORDS

Seattle, Washington
Portland, Oregon
Denver, Colorado
Vancouver, B.C.
Scottsdale, Arizona
Minneapolis, Minnesota

Peanut Butter Publishing
2925 Fairview Avenue East
Seattle, Washington 98102
877-728-8837
info@peanutbutterpublishing.com

Acknowledgments

While there were many people who assisted in putting together *In Our Own Words...*, Washington NARAL and the editor would gratefully like to thank writer and activist Bette Gall-Vaughn, Marcie Bloom and Rachel Perlmutter of Aradia Women's Health Center, and Dr. Suzanne Poppema of Aurora Medical Services especially for their contributions. Andrew Roth, interning in NARAL's office, was an immense help in proofing and checking each story. Thank you also to Stephanie Gabriel at Peanut Butter Publishing for her enthusiasm and suggestions for this project. It was Karen Cooper of Washington NARAL who had the dream of doing such a book and we would like to thank Elliott Wolf for helping this dream come to fruition.

Update January 2008 printing
Ten years have passed since the original publication of *In Our Own Words...*, and while much has changed since then, the powerful stories on these pages continue to resonate today. In addition to those individuals and institutions recognized above, we would like to thank all of the activists, volunteers, interns, staff, board members, and donors who have stood up for women everywhere and continued to fight for the right to choose.

Special Thanks

Board of Directors
Claudia Arana
Jack Burg
Councilmember Richard Cole
Janeen Comenote
Suone Cotner
Sue Evans
Edie Gilliss
Sierra Hansen
Shakti Hawkins
Trudi Inslee
Susan Landon
Representative Liz Loomis
Norma Miller
Geoff Patrick
Michelle Quackenbush
Peter Sagerson
Vandana Slatter
Ben Vaught
Eileen Weinstein

Honorary Council
Kenneth Alhadeff
Dr. Ellsworth and
    Nancy Alvord
Eileen Gibbons, M.D.
Rosalinda Guillen
George Heidorn and
    Margaret Rothschild
Gregory Hullender
Stewart Jay, Esq.
Martha Kongsgaard
Governor Gary Locke
Judith Lonnquist, Esq.
Carol Pencke
Carrie Rhodes
Pepper Schwartz, Ph.D.
Frank Shoichet, Esq.
King County Executive
    Ron Sims
Rick Steves
Senator Pat Thibaudeau

Preface

Abortion is a topic that usually elicits a strong response. No one tends to feel ambivalent about abortion and there is no greater group of people who feel more strongly about it than those who have been intimately involved with it, in one form or another.

This collection was compiled from letters, poems, thoughts and essays which WA NARAL, the Washington affiliate of the National Abortion and Reproductive Rights Action League, has received throughout the years. Because of the personal nature of their contents, the names have been withheld to protect the contributors. In going through them while working on this project, I found myself confronted with my own conflicting emotions, from grief for the most abused of these women to rage at a system that would allow such atrocities. Several times I was moved to tears from the sheer power of the strength, courage and fortitude shown by these women.

From the writings of women who experienced the terror, pain and humiliation of illegal abortions before *Roe v. Wade* to the strong, confident voices of the women who have had a legal choice, all of the contributors to *In Our Own Words…* share the same message: *We Must Not Go Back!*

– Elizabeth Lake
Editor

Introduction

It is now 35 years since the U.S. Supreme Court ruled on the side of women's rights and health in its January 22, 1973 *Roe v. Wade* decision. The ruling ushered in a new era for American women: one in which women finally had access to safe, legal abortion care.

As some of the stories in this collection starkly illustrate, before women had the right to choose, all too many suffered humiliation, permanent injury and death in filthy, dangerous places. These women's stories are heartbreaking to read, and serve as powerful reminders of why we continue to fight to protect the right to choose so many years later. We must never go back to the days before *Roe*.

Even now, a woman's right to choose is continually threatened, both physically and politically, by anti-choice and anti-woman forces. Since *Roe*, there have been over 5,600 acts of violence including 174 counts of arson, 41 bombings, 4 kidnappings and 7 deaths. Every day, threats and harassment affect about one-third of U.S. abortion clinics and the women who need their services.

Bolstered by conservative elected officials and federal judges, anti-choice extremists have made considerable inroads since 1973. By chipping away at the right to choose on the state and federal levels, the radical right has succeeded in placing increased burdens on women's ability to access the full range of reproductive health care.

The Hyde Amendment, first passed by Congress in 1976 and still in effect today, prohibits federal funds from being used for abortion care, except in cases of rape, incest, or when the woman's life is in danger. Women in federal prisons and many poor women dependent on Medicaid funds are refused abortions, and all women who work for the federal government are forbidden from choosing

a health insurance policy that covers abortion. Congress likewise denies abortion coverage for military personnel and their families.

In the states, countless laws have been considered and passed that rein in a woman's right to choose. These laws range from mandatory waiting periods and biased counseling requirements to outright abortion bans. In 2006, South Dakota passed a complete abortion ban, without an exception for the health or safety of the woman. Thankfully, the people of South Dakota mobilized in response, and overturned the ban on a ballot referendum that fall. Yet state legislatures across the country are working to enact similar bans.

One of the most far-reaching changes that has taken place since *Roe* is the conservative take-over of the U.S. Supreme Court. This fact hit home in April 2007, when the Court voted 5-4 to uphold the Federal Abortion Ban. The ban prohibits certain abortion procedures used as early as the 12th week of pregnancy, and has no exception for the health of the woman. Furthermore, it trumps any state laws providing more protection for a woman's right to choose.

Despite these anti-choice successes, Washington remains a strongly pro-choice state. We at NARAL Pro-Choice Washington understand how crucial the right to choose is to women's health. Women's ability to determine what happens to our bodies is at the foundation of women's freedom. The proceeds from every copy of this book go directly to support the work of NARAL Pro-Choice Washington, dedicated to using the political process to guarantee and protect every woman's right to choose.

Karen S. Cooper

– Karen S. Cooper
Executive Director
NARAL Pro-Choice Washington
January 2008

IN OUR
OWN WORDS

This disclosure is not easy for me. Basically, I'm a private person. Despite the passage of 24 years since my illegal abortion, it takes no effort for me to recall in graphic detail the fear and agony I experienced.

I was 18 and away from home at college when I became pregnant. I had grown up in a protective, very restrictive environment in which my parents never mentioned sex, let alone birth control. When I found myself pregnant, my world felt as if it had collapsed. I knew I was not ready for a child. I was positive that my strict father would disown me if he found out. I wanted to continue going to school. Abortion seemed the only workable option for me.

At that time it was incredibly difficult to locate a medical doctor willing to perform abortions. My best friend and I spent weeks tracking down every possible lead, including all sorts of futile home remedies which were supposed to induce abortions. In my desperation I was ready to submit my body to one of the "back-alley" abortionists we had found, but my friend insisted that we wait until we could find a medical doctor with, at the minimum, a clean office.

We eventually located "Wilson", the underground abortion network's code name for a Washington, D. C. area obstetrician-gynecologist, whose patient population consisted heavily of the daughters, lovers or wives of politicians. I was told that I had to come alone and I was blind-folded on the trip from the airport to his office. With a lot of help from my friends, I was able to come up with the $500 Wilson charged back in 1961. Wilson was gentle, sensitive, and he had the only clean office I had seen in my search. I was grateful that I had found him. I can remember sitting in his waiting room, fantasizing about what I would do with the rest of my life.

After a physical exam, Wilson told me that my pregnancy was already well into the second trimester and that he could not chance an abortion in his office. Nor could he hospitalize me and perform a therapeutic abortion, as my life was not at stake. It had taken me so long to find Wilson,

9

and now he couldn't help me. He sat there as I cried. After a few minutes he told me that he was arranging to send me to Baltimore where he knew of a woman who did later-stage abortions. He warned me to tell her I had only $200 and to hide the rest of my money. As I left his office, he pushed a vial of penicillin into my hand, admonishing me to begin taking them at once and to continue for ten days, to ward off infection.

In Baltimore I was met at the train station and led to a dilapidated brownstone. Inside was the abortionist, a woman dressed totally in black, watching television and drinking straight from a bottle of Canadian Club. The little courage I had left vanished rapidly.

She led me to a table in her dining room, speaking to me only to haggle over her fee.

After Wilson's comforting ways, I felt totally abandoned and very frightened. Yet I chose to proceed rather than remain pregnant.

There was no pretense that this was a medical office. No sterile drape to cover me. No gloves for the abortionist.

She refused to answer my questions about the procedure. Her method of abortion was to insert a catheter into my uterus which would subsequently result in contractions to expel the catheter as well as the fetus. In other words, I would go into labor.

For the next 48 hours I was alone in a locked room in her attic. The room contained an iron bed with no sheets, a chair, two magazines and a toilet. I was brought no food or water. I had never felt so alone or terrified in my life. I kept wondering if I would ever make it out that room. I was painfully aware that only Wilson and the two women knew where I was.

Despite my fears of being raped or murdered, I did finally fall asleep that first night. All the next day I waited for something to start happening in my body, but nothing did.

Somehow I managed to fall asleep again that next night, only to awaken to violent cramping. I saw blood all over the bed. The pain was excruciating. I didn't know if I was in labor or dying. I crawled to the toilet, feeling an overwhelming urge to push. I heard screams, but did not recognize that they were coming from me. There was more pushing and then a release of something. Then more pain and too much blood. Something was stuck ... I tore at the placenta, trying desperately to free it.

With dry sobs, I crawled back to bed.

I woke up to someone shaking me very hard. The woman who had met me at the station was angry with me.

"Get up and get out of here!" she yelled. "Look at the big mess you made!"

As I slowly dressed, I looked around the room and couldn't believe all the blood I saw.

I felt weak and very cold. I shivered and dug my hands into my pockets, feeling the vial Wilson had given me. He didn't want to risk performing my abortion himself, but it was OK for him to send me to this place as long as he could assuage his guilt with a little penicillin.

For years I had nightmares focused on that terrifying weekend in Baltimore when I was eighteen. My back-alley abortion was indeed horrendous, but I was, after all, one of the lucky ones. I lived. But I *never* forgot ... and that is why I feel so strongly that safe, legal abortion must remain a choice for all women.

When I was a teenager in about 1940, I baby-sat the two children of a lovely young divorced woman named Helen. She had few employable skills, an exhausting, poorly paid job and her ex-husband only occasionally made child-support payments. Suddenly she died ....

The children came to live with me and my family for a few weeks while custody was sorted out. The six-year-old curled up in my arms and talking about their mother's death. He said, "Momma just bled and bled and we couldn't help her."

I was too young to guess what that might mean. Several years later my mother told me that Helen had died of a botched abortion attempt. She impressed upon me what a sorrowful and serious choice an abortion would be, but that it should be safe and legal because sometimes it was the best alternative.

The children were raised by their father, a sweet irresponsible alcoholic, and a series of stepmothers. The girl had a terrible, tumultuous adolescence, but after several children and a broken marriage, is a stable wonderful middle-aged woman. The boy was killed in a gambling accident.

I think society would have been much better served if Helen could have had a safe, legal abortion and raised her two children herself.

While I did not have an abortion, I believe my story illustrates exactly what we do not want to go back to before women legally had the right to decide for themselves if and when they would have children.

I became pregnant on New Year's in 1966, before abortions were legal. I was a senior in high school, and I was still a "practicing Catholic." The father in my case was of no help and I was terrified of my parents' reaction, so I hid my pregnancy from them until I was six months along and they confronted me a week before graduation. Had the school authorities found out, I would have been kicked out of school, although I was an honor student.

My father verbally and physically assaulted me in the confrontation before kicking me out of the family household. My mother was mortified that anyone else would find out.

A girlfriend's mother made arrangements for me to stay at an unwed mother's home in Seattle, hidden in the Central area, operated by the Catholic Charities. I knew nothing of my rights or options, legal or otherwise, nor did the social worker at Catholic Charities give me any. There was no "informed consent." I was told that the girls (and women) at the home were not allowed to do anything in preparation for keeping their babies. I was told the only option was signing adoption papers. My parents did not want to see me again or allow me back home until I had given away my baby. When I protested and told the social worker I did not want to give up my baby, I was told that if I didn't sign the papers, they could and would take her away from me anyway and I would never see her. She simply would live in foster homes instead of a permanent home. I had *no choice.*

My anger and grief have not subsided to this day. I miss my daughter daily. She is now eighteen, the same age I was when she was born. I want to make sure that she and all other women in this country continue to have choices and options fully available to them in matters of reproduction,

from sex education to birth control services, from abortion to adoption services. This should also include a full range of services available to young or poor parents who wish to keep their children. Having to give your child away because you are poor and without resources is obscene.

Being told that even thinking about sex is a mortal sin for which you'll go to hell and that using birth control is another mortal sin on top of that is also obscene. It simply leads to more unplanned pregnancies. Punishing women for having sex by forcing them to continue unplanned pregnancies and them forcing them to give up their babies through adoption is cruelty beyond comprehension. I deserved better; my daughter deserves better; we all deserve a choice.

This is the last straw. Finally, I'm mad, *angry mad!* My tolerance is gone. I am not now, or ever have been, a pro-abortionist. Being one of the apparently all too silent majority, I haven't rammed my beliefs down anyone's throat. But I'm sick and tired of the so-called pro-lifers who are fanatically busy doing just that. Pro-life what? Make sure every fertilized ovum gets born and after that "the hell with them?" When each and every pro-life advocate feeds and gives tender, loving care to a bloated, starving, beaten, neglected child in the world, I'll sure listen to them. If they are going to manipulate destiny, then they should follow through. If they are as vocal about promoting contraception as they are screaming about baby murderers, I'll listen, too. What a bunch of hypocrites!

I have a true story to tell which made an indelible impression on my life, and explains some of my feelings. As a very young and naive student nurse at the University of Colorado, I witnessed an eleven-year-old child, who was admitted in agonizing labor. She looked like a balloon with attached head, arms, and legs. She died, the baby was dead, and her father went to prison. Who were the criminals? Wouldn't an early abortion have been the most merciful answer?

I would like to have Dottie Roberts of Lake Stevens in Snohomish County answer that. (She beat back an attempt to amend the Republican anti-abortion plank to permit public money to pay for abortions in cases of rape or incest.) The Washington Republican Party platform is a disaster. Weren't there any courageous, responsible, socially conscious members there who aren't Reagan clones? I was a Republican, but this is so sickening, I'm not sure what I am now.

Will the silent majority please start speaking up before the idiots take over the world?

"Every time one makes a choice, there is a loss. If I choose "A" over "B", I lose "B". Even if it is the correct choice, I still experience loss. Therefore it is important to have permission to grieve, even with a good choice."

— Eileen Gibbons, M. D.

Even fifteen years later, this story is hard to tell; not because I'm sorry I had an illegal abortion, but because even now, I find it hard to forgive myself for being so stupid as to allow myself to get into a situation where I would need an abortion. It was the spring of 1970; I was 33, almost 34, in the fifth year of my second marriage. I had children, 10, 8, and 5. The marriage was deteriorating and in spite of myself I was becoming older but wiser.

I had at long last been accepted into the Graduate School of Education at the University of Washington after having spent a year taking classes to increase my grade point so the committee would be convinced that I was serious in my desire to get a Masters Degree in Guidance and Counseling. My husband knew that I wanted to go to graduate school, but he began lobbying for me to have another child. He told my family I was being uncooperative, and wouldn't let me get out of bed to get my diaphragm, saying I should be able to handle going to graduate school with three children and a newborn. I knew I couldn't but he kept pushing and then I got pregnant.

I would wake out of a sound sleep in the middle of the night and pace the floor – trying to decide what to do. A friend of mine had told me in confidence that she had gone to Canada and had an abortion. I decided that was the only way, and somehow I would cover my time away from home, get to Canada, get it done, and return. When I talked further with the woman, she told me that there was another physician in Seattle who performed abortions, so I made an appointment with him. I told him I was in graduate school, that my husband must not know what I was doing, but I had made up my mind.

We arranged to meet after his office had closed for the day. I don't remember how long it took, but I got off the table, drove home, fixed my family's dinner, told my husband I had a blazing headache (which wasn't true, but I felt very weak), and went to bed. I got up and went to class the next morning, though I walked very slowly and sat down

very carefully. The doctor had instructed me to call his office if there were any complications, and thankfully I didn't have to. I paid him $500 — $200 I borrowed from savings accounts begun for the children by my parents, and $300 I borrowed from a member of my family to whom I will always be grateful. It took me two years of weekly holding back some money out of the groceries to pay back the children and my benefactor, so I had a constant reminder what had happened, but I never regretted my decision. Shortly after the operation, the same doctor fitted me with an IUD and I breathed many sighs of relief.

Two years ago, I watched the film *Educating Rita*, and felt such a sense of immediate empathy for the woman whose husband flushed her birth control pills down the toilet and burned her school books in the backyard. I had never felt necessarily alone, I just had never seen my life portrayed on the screen before.

Would it have mattered had the abortion been legal? Yes, in so many ways. It wouldn't have cost so much, but I still would have had to hide it from my husband. I was lucky. I had a network, which included a friend with vital information, and it was done by a caring physician. Do I feel bad about the tissue I aborted? No. Since that time, I have read much about spirituality – about the concept of the continuity of the soul – the variability of the times and conditions under which the soul "attaches" to the physical body. Particularly helpful has been the work of noted social scientist, Helen Wambach (*Life Before Life, Reliving Past Lives*), who has regressed thousands of people to find that the soul is an energy which is not consumed by the body, but uses the body as a vehicle to manifest in the physical world. I have personally been through past-life regression several times, and I know that there is much there to be learned to benefit me in this life.

To have an abortion was a severe and drastic learning experience for me. With all my intelligence and education, it took such a severe experience to teach me about the value of my own life – the need to stand up and be responsible for

my own life and have respect for myself, above and beyond any role I might be living. Though I will never experience that again in this life, it took the growth of that tissue to impress the lesson on me. I do understand, and in the writing of this, I can now find the love to forgive myself.

My children know this story. They are now old enough to understand. Not that they might not have their own experience to finally get a message which is personal to their own individual lives, but my daughters now know that the option of a legal abortion is one that is available. I would hope, with their knowledge of my experience, they would never put themselves in a position to learn the lesson as I did; but if they do, I will be there to help them learn to love themselves, forgive, and move on. They also know that I have never regretted being a vehicle for their lives.

1997   Roe V Wade has been legal in the United States for almost 25 years.
Roe V Wade keeps abortion legal, yet 80% of U.S. counties have NO abortion provider.

1959   In a small town in a western state, abortion is not legal. The term, "battered wife" was not yet a phrase.
Nor was there the term, or any law addressing "Domestic Violence."

Marcia and I had known one another since grade school. Yet we didn't become close friends until we both had married, given birth to children, and bowled on the same league.

Marcia was barely 5 feet tall, barely weighed 100 pounds, just a bit of a woman. She had married one of the football players, big and burly, he made five or six of her! She had two children at the time we met again ... I had four.

There was very little we didn't share with one another. We spoke on the phone several times each day, took our kids to the park, went skating, and were at each other's homes several times each week.

The first signs of abuse I noticed were some serious bruises on her arm. She gave some justification ... and I believed her. More and more often, when we would be on the phone, I would hear her husband in the background, using loud and abusive language, at times demanding she "Hang up that fucking phone before I knock you across the room."

Yes, George had come home drunk again. And he had beaten her again.

It was not long after that when Marcia broke down and confided everything to me .... I was not a battered wife at this time, yet knew many women who were ... those my age, my mother's age, my grandmother's age. Law, church and tradition dictated that we be submissive ... don't make

waves ... don't "air dirty laundry in public." There were dozens of sayings, laws and traditions protecting the abusive male.

There were NO laws protecting women.

I began to help Marcia plan her escape from this violent household before he killed her or her two children. The youngest would be starting school the next year and she would be better able to support herself and the kids.

We had planned, worked a day-at-a-time finding ways to save money on this and that ... pricing small apartments.

Marcia was rigid about putting her diaphragm in before having sex ... she didn't dare refuse George anything! And he had threatened her about ever "getting pregnant again!"

One morning the phone rang ... at first I didn't even recognize Marcia's voice ... yet I was able to understand her plea for help. I raced over to her home where I found this tiny friend of mine with her lip swollen, her eyes beginning to blacken ... she was limping. He had come home very late the night before ... very drunk, beat her and raped her.

The next month she missed her period. And the next month discovered he had impregnated her during the brutal beating and rape.

At this point "SHE" had NO CHOICE!!!!

If she remained pregnant she would be forced to remain with George, which could mean death to herself, the fetus, and the two children.

Marcia was like a desperate and injured animal .... I can't even remember how we obtained the name of an abortion provider but we did. This provider was 300 miles away ... it was in the middle of a frigid winter ... and there was no one to get money needed for the abortion. Marcia's parents were both dead. And, because this was an ILLEGAL procedure, we couldn't tell or ask just anyone.

Marcia was discussing this with me on the phone when, unknown to her, an uncle had walked into her house

and overheard the conversation. He blackmailed Marcia by stating "HE" would give her the money for the abortion if she would have SEX WITH HIM. His own niece!!

If we all were honest, just how many times have we traded sex for less???

We started out early one morning, just Marcia and I, driving in a blinding snowstorm ... whiteouts at times where the dividing line in the highway was covered over ... few cars on the road. At that point I doubt ANYTHING could have turned us back!!

Directions led us to an alley where rickety wooden steps led up one flight to the doctor's office door. He smelled of liquor and body odor and his medical jacket was stained. He told me to go back downstairs and wait in the car.

About an hour later , Marcia returned to the car in pain, clutching her abdomen and sobbing. We grieved, yet never once doubted her decision! Miraculously we drove through the storm and I dropped her off at her home. George was out of town on a two-week job.

Early next morning the phone rang. Marcia was in a panic ... bleeding ... and I rushed to take her to the hospital. They were able to stop the bleeding and gave her the following, albeit, unbelievable and shocking news, "You can go home now ... and the baby is just fine."

BABY ????? How could this be ?? Marcia had gone through hell-on-earth ... had traded sex for money for this abortion ... had given that money to the doctor ... WHAT HAD HE DONE ! ! ! Was the BABY partially mutilated or ? or ? or ? WHAT WAS HAPPENING INSIDE HER!!!!!

Every second of every minute of every day of every week of every month for the next 7 and 1/2 months were tortuous for Marcia. Again forced to remain with this abusive man AND grotesque mind-pictures of the growing baby she carried within her, life was a torment unknown to few.

Her son was born perfectly normal. He was named Jeffrey. Marcia was finally able to leave the abusive household when Jeffrey was two years old. She had to leave

town with her children and very little else.

For the next 18 years, whenever Jeffrey happened to be late from school, Marcia went into a panic ... expecting to be "punished by God" ... or maybe George had kidnapped him ... or ? ?

When Jeffrey went into the Army her fears increased. Marcia has relaxed a little now, as Jeffrey has married and has children of his own.

The above is one of the millions of stories of INDIVIDUAL lives, INDIVIDUAL reasons, INDIVIDUAL pain of an unwanted pregnancy.

Thankfully, Roe V Wade is, so far, still legal.

Government never gives us anything they haven't already taken away ... and they are close to taking reproductive freedom away from women once again.

— Bette Gall-Vaughn
11/19/97

Bette Gall-Vaughn is a successful writer and activist who has survived incest, rape and an abusive marriage. She is also a mother, stepmother and a grandmother. She is pro-choice AND pro-life.

"I believe that the abortion issue can never regress to a
point where it would be made illegal again. Too many
women — and a lot of men — simply wouldn't stand for it.
It's too well accepted. Too many women have had to use it
in their times of need. Too many women have discovered
that their politics change when their situations change; and
though they may have once thought abortion was wrong,
they are persuaded to a prochoice position when the need
arises for them or a loved one to end an unwanted
pregnancy."

— From *Why I Am An Abortion Doctor*
by Suzanne T. Poppema, M.D.

In the 1920's my step-aunt wound up permanently in a wheelchair after her husband insisted she have an illegal abortion.

In the 1960's I went to college in Arizona. Women sought help to terminate unwanted pregnancies by traveling across the border into Mexico. One close friend went to Mexico and unknowingly came back still pregnant. She then married and their child was born severely deformed. It was suggested the deformity was due to the unsuccessful Mexican "abortion". Another dear friend developed an infection following a Mexican abortion and will never have children.

In the 1980's my husband and I had an unplanned, yet welcomed son. Three years later our marriage was unstable. I chose a legal abortion. My husband was by my side and helped me through the grief process. We have had two more children since then. They were both very wanted, though both unplanned.

I do not want my daughter or my sons to ever have to risk their own or another's health by having no choice but a Mexican or "back-alley" abortion. I want grandchildren, but I want my grandchildren healthy and by their parents' choice.

Unwanted Children

Jim is now a grown man in body but his mind is that of a child. His parents were brother and sister. His mother was 15 years old when he was born. He was put in foster care as an infant where he screamed night and day. His related parental genes combined to present numerous problems. Only the special care of a special person helped him to survive to adulthood. Adulthood presented more problems than even this special person could handle and after complaints from the neighbors, Jim was institutionalized. There he will remain for the rest of his life with overnight weekend passes if he has been 'good' for a certain length of time. The cost of his care is borne by the taxpayers while he bears the hurt of his unfortunate parentage.

Stephanie is almost a year old now. She arrived in foster care directly from the hospital when there was little hope that she could ever see or hear, her digestive system was in confusion, her head bent awkwardly to one side, her brain encased in a skull too small. With round-the-clock special care, she has survived. Her head is still bent and special therapy is given for that and to help develop the little bit of eyesight she has. Her seizures from her too small skull and digestive problems are controlled by special food and large doses of expensive medicine. Her cries are just whimpers as she goes on from day to day. Whatever caused her condition, Stephanie was not wanted and her capability of enjoying life is slim indeed.

Parents, children and taxpayers deserve a choice.

I was a young country girl when I married. It was a marriage of convenience as our two families and my future husband pushed me into it despite my reluctance to enter into a marriage with this man.

I planned not to have any children for at least two years, however, I did not know how to avoid pregnancy. My husband did not want to use a condom. I immediately became pregnant. I was determined not to have this child as I was simply not ready to assume this responsibility. I did everything I could think of such as drink an entire bottle of castor oil, hours of jumping rope and finally ending up with a glass of Lysol disinfectant, from which I barely recovered. I ultimately delivered a little boy. By this time I knew this marriage would never work as we were of two completely different personalities. He turned out to be shiftless and turned to heavy gambling.

I soon found I was pregnant again. This time I was determined that I would not bring another child into the world fathered by this man. I knew that I would eventually have to bring up any children that I had without benefits from my husband and I was prepared to go to any limits to prevent this pregnancy. I even tried to choke myself to death, only to have horribly bloodshot eyes for several days afterward.

Finally I heard of a woman who controlled her family by the use of a catheter and through a friend she wrote down explicit instructions – *and it worked.* At least one time I had to resort to a knitting needle as the catheter did not seem to work. Since in this small town there was no better method, I continued to use this method until I learned of better ways which would prevent conception.

During this time I was the sole provider for my child. I was inexperienced so I did housework and I grew full of resentment – mostly at my husband for not protecting me. We eventually separated at my request. I had to place my little boy in foster homes and there was a battle going on within me as I could not make ends meet. I was constantly

in debt and just having a rough time of it in general. The problems grew bigger and bigger and the little boy grew more difficult to handle.

One of the main reasons I did not want to have a child in the first place was that both my husband and I had quite bad acne as well as similar other problems. I felt that a child born of us would surely be afflicted with these problems. Sure enough – they began to show up at an early age and they plagued him for the rest of his life. My heart ached for him and I felt I had betrayed him by passing on these problems to him. The older he got the worse the problems became and there were many years of absolute hell for both of us. He tried to take his life many times. For years each time the phone rang I dreaded answering it, fearing the worst until finally when he was 42 years of age, he ended his tortured life.

Needless to say I have lived a life filled with guilt and remorse. Unfortunately I am on a limited income and can help very little. I just hope that no little boy has to be born to endure what my son had to. And that no woman has to go through what I did. The availability of an abortion would have made such a difference. He was never happy, nor was I. *Every woman should have the right to choose when to have her babies.*

In February, 1981, I had an abortion. I was married, and 24 years old. Having an abortion is an emotionally painful and difficult experience to go through. It is not a decision that is made easily. It is not an action that a woman, or a couple, take lightly.

At the time I had the abortion, 4 years ago, I realized how grateful I was that it was a possible course of action. Until I was faced with a pregnancy I could not carry to term, I was not aware of how important, how vital this option is to so many women.

I was especially fortunate to be able to go to a special abortion clinic that provided good care, good follow up, and counseling. I was cared for by people trained in this procedure. In light of the emotional stress that I experienced at that time, I cannot emphasize enough how very valuable it was to have trained professionals, in a reputable clinic, to care for me.

In retrospect, years later, and emotionally healed, I cannot stop being grateful for the fact that I was able to obtain an abortion. I have since become divorced, and this is a major factor in my feelings of relief and thankfulness that I was able to decide NOT to have a child. I always feel that not only was one life spared from growing up in an unhappy home, or a life with divorced parents, but indeed due to my abortion MY OWN LIFE WAS SAVED. Had I not had the abortion, I may never have gotten divorced due to the added factor of having a child to consider.

I am white, Jewish, and I come from an upper-middle class family. I never finished college, and I married at the age of eighteen. I am now back in college, obtaining a degree in Yiddish culture. I am endlessly grateful for what I consider to be this second chance in my life. This "second chance" is directly related to the option I had to have an abortion. As a result, divorced and childless, I am able to begin again, to renew, and rejuvenate, and add to the world as a productive human being.

Abortions save lives.

I had been doing drugs and living with addicts when I realized I was pregnant. I told my boyfriend I wanted to try to get an abortion. We were driving at the time and he pulled over abruptly, hit me a few times and pushed me out of the car. Needless to say, this was the end of our relationship. I was not yet eighteen and was too confused and mixed up to have a baby. I knew I did not want to be pregnant. I didn't, however, know what to do about it. I remember punching myself in the stomach to "make it go away."

Through friends, I found out about a doctor who did abortions. I was a few months overdue by then. I went to him with high hopes and he examined me. He turned out to be a sexual deviant who loved to give pelvics and molested me on the examining table. I then went to another "back alley" doctor who gave me drugs and referred me to another doctor who would perform the abortion. I went alone that day. I remember going into a bathroom across from his clinic and shooting up some Seconals. I didn't know if it would be painful. I did not know what to expect. I walked into his office only to be thrown out after being told I was too far along. He did give me the name of another doctor. I was an emotional wreck at this point and called a friend who picked me up and took me to the fourth doctor. Luckily this man was a gem. I was in such a state when I came into his office. He was kind and gentle. I later found out this same man was instrumental in changing Hawaii's abortion laws with his support. He counseled me to clean myself up, which I did, and finally was able to tell my parents who, to my surprise, became very supportive. My father wanted me to have the child, however, my mother thought the abortion would be best. We got the consent of my previous therapist and went through all the legal maneuverings to obtain a therapeutic abortion.

The day finally came (by that time the baby was kicking) and I was feeling some motherly instincts. I was so confused. I just wanted everything to be over. I was prepped in the hospital and wheeled into the room where the abortion

was to be performed. The doctor (this was yet another doctor) came in, examined me and said no way ... I was too far along. There I was, legs spread apart, shaved, the nightmare finally seemingly over, and once again my whole world collapsed. I can't tell you what was going through my head at the time. I've blocked a lot of this out. The pain, frustration, uncertainty and knowledge of what I had done to my body with drugs before finding myself pregnant welled up in me and were too much to bear. There was no other option but to have the baby and give it up for adoption. This meant more legalities, more papers to sign. Meanwhile the "father" was trying to legally get custody of this unborn child. He was still a junkie, he was crazy and I knew that no child would benefit from him in his state.

I grew more and more motherly toward this thing growing in me. I was living at home and in the care of my parents. Somehow, this whole experience had brought us closer. I was off drugs and back to getting my health, mental and spiritual state in order.

My world fell apart once again. I went into labor at six months. The kindly doctor who had helped set things up for my "legal abortion" delivered my baby. It was frightening. My father drove me to the hospital since my mother was in the military hospital at the time. I was separated from my father and put into this cold, barren room on a cold metal table. All I could hear were the screams and moans of other women in labor. The nurse was nasty to me, cold and heartless. Only my doctor was kind and comforting. I gave birth to a tiny one pound 10 ounce little boy. He cried and lived. I was happy. Two days later he died, and a part of me died with him.

Since this whole experience, my life has been on the upswing. The kindly doctor quoted my case in his fight to help get abortion legalized in the state of Hawaii. I felt my pain and suffering helped pave the way for others so that they would never have to experience the traumatic, horrible things I went through.

Planned Parenthood, NARAL and others have helped set up educational programs to assist young adults in making that choice. It is a painful choice, yet sometimes it is the right choice and it must remain there for us to make. No words can describe the degradation, pain, suffering and horror I went through. I would never wish that on any woman.

I hope my experience helps in some way. It was terrifying, yet I do not feel any guilt. So much of my pain could have been avoided and today, others have the choice to avoid that pain. But that choice must not be taken away from us. Thank you for caring.

Gravida

From the beginning,
I knew you couldn't stay
But every cell
Of my primal being
Welcomed you
To this warm citadel
And outside that place
The hag of reason
Railed and warned
And caused my perfidy
Until
I sent you away
In a cascade of water
And I always sorrowed
And I always wondered
Who you were.

My father was a pharmacist in Seattle during the 50's and 60's. I asked him if any women ever asked him where to go for an abortion – or if he had any stories to tell about it. He said that yes, he regularly referred women to a doctor but he remembered a young teenage girl in particular. She was pregnant by incest with her uncle and went to an apartment building for an abortion. My dad said that the apartment had blood all over – like she was "butchered." It was an unsafe abortion to say the least and my dad never did find out if she lived or died. He supports legal abortion because he knew too many women who had to go through the frightening, degrading, and sometimes deadly illegal abortions.

It was 1969, I was 21, living on my own, working, and going to college when I got pregnant. My boyfriend would not even discuss marriage. Both his best friend and his brother had married because a baby had been on the way and they were unhappy. He was not going to subject a child to that sort of situation.

He and a pre-med student discussed trying to get me to abort on our own using Quinine. Thankfully an alternative developed.

Through a friend, we found out about a midwife in another city who would perform abortions (they were illegal then). The next weekend I was on my way with another woman I had never met before, one who had an abortion previously and another young woman who was pregnant.

First we made contact with a R. N. who gave us some antibiotics to take afterward. Then on to Lupe's house in a poor section of town. The other woman was too far along for the abortion so that left me. My boyfriend was to pick me up the next day. Lupe inserted a catheter into my cervix and packed me full of gauze. I spent the night like this in a tiny room, Lupe asked me to be quiet because she was having company over. I could hear them laughing and talking while I sat alone, terrified.

The next morning Lupe performed the abortion – basically a dilation and curretage with no anesthetic. It was incredibly painful. I can remember trying not to cry out with the tears streaming down my face.

Of course it makes me sad to remember it all, but I know that I was in no position to be raising a child back then. I also know that it would have been impossible to have given away a baby.

I am 37 now. I have a happy marriage and a beautiful baby boy for whom I thank God every day. Parenting is a job that one should be ready for and committed to. Sixteen years ago I wasn't even close.

I was in my middle thirties, a housewife with four children, when I separated from my husband of sixteen years and took steps to terminate a marriage characterized by emotional and physical abuse.

Shortly after the announcement of my filing for divorce appeared in the newspaper's vital statistics column, I was invited out for dinner by a colleague of my husband's, who had separated from his wife just a half year before. I was very naïve and thought this would be a pleasant evening. I knew the man in question and considered him pleasant. It was my first date in over seventeen years.

The evening was extremely hot, and the area where I live does not air-condition most homes or businesses. We had a very pleasant dinner, I thought, but the heat was oppressive. My date suggested that we go to his home and sit out in his backyard. It was still early in the evening and daylight.

In my innocence I saw nothing sinister in his suggestion, and maybe he had no ulterior motive. We had had a before-and-after dinner drink and wine with our meal. He continued to drink more wine and, after it got dark, made a few passes.

I did not take this seriously and saw his advances as harmless. Maybe because of the drinks I had, I wasn't using good judgment. He suggested we go back into the house, and I unthinkingly acquiesced.

When we got inside, he steered me down the hall, where to my horror I saw he was pointing me to the bedroom. I grabbed the sides of the doorway with my hands, but he pushed me in and threw me onto the bed. I now realized I was in trouble and started to beg him. "Please don't do this to me," I repeated hysterically. He ignored my pleading and raped me.

Afterwards he told me that he "could tell I wanted it." I was too stunned and in shock to do anything and was not aggressive by nature. It seemed incredible that this had happened to me with someone I had known as well as I knew

47

this man. I had never had sex with anyone except my husband.

Later on in life, when my anger surfaced and I was able to confront him, he denied that a rape had occurred, because "I didn't struggle hard enough — I should have run away from him, etc. etc." To this day he has not admitted that I was date-raped.

When I found myself pregnant after this experience, it was such a relief to know that safe, legal, and inexpensive abortion was available to me. I found sympathy and understanding from the health department in my community, and I was able to obtain a discreet abortion five weeks after the incident.

I am so grateful that I wasn't forced to continue the pregnancy or required to try to convince some skeptical panel that I had been raped. It would have been hard to prove, not to say humiliating, considering that I was on a date with my assailant, that I had known him for some time, that I was in his home, this man was a respected professional, and that we were both mature adults. I shudder at the damage this affair could have done to my children, particularly my teen-aged daughter, at a sensitive and vulnerable age. My husband was being very vindictive at the time, and would have used this pregnancy in devastating ways to get back at me.

Thank God I had a choice!

Seven years ago, as a 31-year-old divorced woman with one daughter, I discovered I was pregnant — even though I was using birth control at the time. Since the relationship which led to the pregnancy had ended, and because I had a limited salary on which to raise my existing child and maintain our quality of life, I chose to terminate the pregnancy by abortion. This was not a cold-hearted act — it was simply the best and most logical choice for me to make at that time, as related to my social, mental, and economic health. I did not use abortion as a method of birth control, but rather as a means to terminate an unwanted pregnancy.

Although I'm sure my story is not particularly unusual, I hope it will help to reinforce how important it is to all women to have this choice available — both now and throughout the future. It should not be a political or legal issue, to be debated in legislative sessions or courtrooms. It is a matter of personal freedom and choice — a woman's RIGHT to control her own body.

Our right to choose, guaranteed to us under the Constitution, appears to be in jeopardy. I want to remind all women who feel as I do that this is NOT the time to remain silent. SPEAK OUT AND LET YOUR FEELINGS ON THIS ISSUE BE HEARD! Your right to your own body is at stake.

"The tears are the healing ...
they are not the pain."

— Anonymous

My Abortion Story

by Elizabeth Furse
U.S. Representative from Oregon

Today is the 24th anniversary of Roe v Wade, but my story begins 12 years earlier in the spring of 1961. I was 25, a wife and mother of two children. My husband and I were thrilled by the news of a third child due in November.

I have never spoken publicly about what happened in the spring of 1961, and it is difficult for me to do so now. For the past 36 years I have been carrying around a painful memory, unknown to even my closest friends. But once again the right to a safe, legal abortion is under attack. Once again women in this country may be forced into the choice I had to make as a young woman.

When I was 2.5 months pregnant, I caught what I first thought was a simple cold, I became quite ill and ran a high fever for two days before being diagnosed with the measles. Subsequent tests confirmed our worst fear. The fetus was badly affected. If I carried my pregnancy to term, my baby would likely be blind, deaf and severely brain damaged.

My husband and I were extremely saddened. We really wanted this baby, however, we thought it would be wrong to carry the pregnancy to term only to bring into the world a life so filled with pain.

We decided to seek an abortion.

My doctor was sympathetic but explained that he would not help because abortion was illegal, and he and I could be prosecuted and jailed for terminating my pregnancy. I was too sad to be outraged.

I knew I could never have an illegal abortion. I had friends who had received illegal abortions. Some had been botched. My husband was a physician who had seen the victims of botched abortions in the emergency room too many times. That was not an option.

My doctor did mention another possibility. Because I only have one kidney, he suggested we might be able to persuade a panel of physicians to recommend terminating the pregnancy because it would place my life in danger. The physicians were willing to recommend an abortion, but only with a total hysterectomy. What a terrible set of choices. I could risk a back-alley abortion, carry a severely brain damaged fetus to term, or lose my fertility forever.

I chose the final option. Instead of being able to have an abortion, I was subjected to major surgery, a hysterectomy, that would forever change my life. The most painful part of the surgery was that it could have been avoided. I returned home to my two beloved children knowing that my family would never become any larger. That decision was made for me by a law so strict that it denied women access to safe health care.

I have a loving husband, two wonderful children and a grandchild who brings me enormous joy. My life is very fulfilling and I look forward and not back. I remain angry, however, that a responsible, loving family was put in the position my family was. We were denied the ability to make the best decision for us.

It is painful for me to speak out about this sad event in my life, but I think it is important. As a member of Congress, I take this life experience with me to the floor of the House of Representatives each time I cast a vote on choice. I have no doubt it is what fuels my fight against extremist attacks on women's reproductive freedom.

During the past 24 years, the discussion and debate over Roe v Wade has become a war of words. What these words lack is a true sense of what women faced before Roe v Wade ensured women the opportunity for safe, rational options in reproductive health.

We must focus on the facts. Abortions will occur. The only question is will they be legal and safe or illegal and unsafe? In my generation, many lives were lost or permanently changed because abortion was not an available medi-

cal option. The young women in this country need to learn a lesson from our pain, We must never give up the fight to keep abortion safe and legal — our lives depend upon it.

— This article is excerpted from *The Oregonian*,
January 22, 1997

You've come a long way baby ...
well, for most it's only MAYBE!
100 years ago, you see,
a law in place, for YOU ... for ME
was "Rule of Thumb," the legal term
for male-made laws ... yeah, brave and firm
and "beat-his-wife"... keep her in line,
then, off to work, him feeling fine.

You've come a long way baby ...
well, for most it remains a MAYBE
Yearly statistics for "INJURY TO WOMEN,"
(not by a stranger ... not skiing or swimming)
DOMESTIC VIOLENCE tops that list
year after year by power of fist
"domestic" violence ... battering
to keep us in line ... don't dance ... don't sing ...
"barefoot and pregnant" to keep us at home
bearing millions of children ... we dare not roam ...
WOMEN and CHILDREN ... keep 'em in line !

Quality of life ?? ah, they're doin' fine.

You've come a long way baby,
UNTRUE for teens
who planned for careers ...
who thought and dreamed.

Dreams snuffed in a minute,
each life now claimed
by LAW ... not CHOICE
their spirits tamed.

For thousands, each year,
not even a maybe
yes, now this "child" is having a baby.

If the CHOICE is to keep it,
it may work out ...
yet, if ENFORCED by men-with-clout
we experience pregnancy
filled with doubt ...
do a duty by LAW,
  by shoulds,
   by shame
while unwanted children "live" the blame ...
The teen gets older ...
does her best ...
few skills for mothering
and no time for rest.

You've come a long way, baby
and statistics agree
most "teen" babies raised in poverty.

You've come a long way, baby.
Well, we'll see
if ROE V. WADE becomes a memory

INDIVIDUAL we are ...
 PERSONAL it must be
I won't choose for you,
nor allow YOUR choice for me!
Take a long, quiet moment,
consider the facts.
Decide for YOURSELF
only YOU can do that.

Are you homeless? helpless?
abused or neglected?
If not, go and help all the little ones affected ...
the "ALREADY BORN"... alive, give THEM voice
while remembering "PRO-CHOICE"
must remain a CHOICE.

—Bette Gall-Vaughn

I very strongly favor the right to be able to have a legal abortion. I do not look kindly on abortion. I can't imagine very many who do. It is a sad thing.

Abortion will go on, legal or not. The difference is a clean sanitary facility with a reputable staff to care for you or a dirty room, unsanitary facilities and a criminal to do the surgery.

I know as I have had both – in a hospital with good care and by a drooling 90 year old man in a filthy suit and a dirty bed. As he was working on me without anything for pain, he said "doesn't feel as good as a big peter does it?"

I also have a girlfriend who died from an abortion on a dirty old mat in a filthy room, her abortion done by a filthy old hag.

Desperate people will do anything.

Please keep abortion legal.

In 1969 I lived in Salt Lake City, Utah. Abortion was not legal there at that time, although it was here in Washington state. Through a friend of mine who was a mid-wife in Washington, I made contact with a physician's office who agreed to take me for an abortion on a certain date. They gave me the instructions on how to get to their office in Bellevue from Sea-Tac airport and, as I recall, had a shuttle car waiting for those of us who had to fly in from out of town.

I left my home in Salt Lake early one morning to fly to Seattle on the pretense of having an interview at the University of Washington. I was a 36 years old, divorced mother of two and working on a Ph.D. I had had one date in six years. Although I was not unattractive, taking care of my children and educating myself for a better life were all I could manage. In 1969, few men would consider a divorced woman with two children, a small income and years of college ahead of her attractive. It is not pertinent, but the bitterness still remains. I was not the one who wanted a divorce and on top of my sense of rejection and desertion, my former husband moved in up the street where he could flaunt his new live-in lover. (And, NOT to help me with my children whom he never saw and never supported.)

That one date led to the unwanted pregnancy that brought me to Seattle for the abortion. I was taken to the doctor's office, was greeted and treated very well. The women responded to my fears and feelings of guilt and shame with smiles and kindness. I was led into the abortion room and prepped. There I first saw the doctor. Every story you have ever heard about doctor's hate for women was personified in this man. My emotions turned immediately from fear to panic, not that I felt my health was in jeopardy, but that he would change his mind and not do the abortion, send me home broke and still pregnant.

As I was prepped for the abortion, I started to cry, not for the baby, but for myself. I'd tried so hard and seemed to be suffering so much and feeling so alone at that moment.

To keep in control, I needed to close my eyes and disassociate myself from what was happening. The physician insulted me continuously saying that after all, I had gotten myself in this mess, that I should be brave enough to take it with my eyes open. As the conversation went on and I began to feel more and more afraid. He finally said if I didn't cooperate with him (open my eyes, talk and smile, I guess) I could just put on my clothes, forget the whole thing and go back where I came from. That is the point where I probably would have done anything he might have requested just to get the procedure over with. I cooperated as best I could and he finished the abortion.

I never want to undergo that kind of humiliation again and I would hope others would not have to go through it either. Though this doctor was performing a legal abortion, he knew that where I came from it wasn't, and I was desperate. With legal abortion in all states, doctors and clinics who perform abortions can set higher standards for its practitioners.

It's hard enough to make the choice of having an abortion and to go through it without adding humiliation and added guilt to the equation. Keep abortion legal everywhere.

Abortion – The Way It Was in 1949

Abortion was, of course, illegal, but if you knew the right people and had the money (in small bills) a way could be found. I had been on my own since before I was 18. I had been asked to leave home because my mother and stepfather had had a child and they felt there was no longer room for me. I was cautioned by my stepfather that if I got pregnant, I needn't bother with any further contact with them or my baby sister.

I lived in two rooms and shared a bath with two other apartments. Many times, at the end of the month, my cooler was bare. I say cooler because I didn't have a refrigerator. I had an ice-box for which I couldn't afford to buy ice. In the winter, I hunkered close to a space heater and listened to the rats run up and down inside the window casings. I fought a continuous invasion of cockroaches. DDT misting bombs cost the enormous sum of $5. In those days I made $115, a month at my job in a bank.

I couldn't even think about a baby – about having a baby. I was too busy trying to stay alive. So when I became pregnant, I knew there was no other option. I had to have an abortion.

My abortion was performed in Seattle – the heretofore "silent ones" will know where it took place, in what building and what doctors were involved (there were four) – bless them! The facilities were clean, the doctor competent; the lack of anesthetic, because of legal consequences, was inhumane. The pain was of a different nature than labor, and in many ways, worse. You couldn't move and you were cautioned not to do so, because it might cause an accident, a perforation of the uterus. I was so frightened, and I shook so badly, that the doctor told me, in a rather brusque way, to compose myself. It cost $250 – more money than I believed to be circulating in the entire world.

It was July and terribly hot for Seattle. I still remember the dress I wore, and how, poor as I was, I could never wear it again. Mostly, I remember feeling numb with fear

and shame over having broken the law; but even more, I was overwhelmed by the enormity of the act itself.

Later, during a marriage of 20 year's duration, I had two children. After each birth, I suffered a post-partum depression. Later still, this was diagnosed as manic-depressive illness and has been chronic for two decades.

This gene was passed to me by my paternal Grandmother, a lady I never met. She was institutionalized at Western State Hospital for some 30 years. She bore one child, my father. In turn I passed this gene to my daughter, who suffers, less severely, from the same condition. One of her youngsters is beginning to show signs of the affliction at age four.

Do I regret my abortion? No. Would I do it again? Of course – though my age precludes the possibility. I will go to bat any day to defend the rights of my little granddaughter – the right to make a decision regarding her genetic legacy – this progenitor of the illustrious, and all too often, the perpetrators of suicide.

Sovereignty over their own bodies is the right of _all_ human beings. The pro-life groups do not understand that by taking away this right of dominion over the body, one's soul is raped and dehumanized. A woman who is forced to bear a child is nothing more than brood stock.

In the years after my abortion, my marriage, and later my divorce, I found that my mother had had three abortions (my father was Catholic and manic-depressive, as well). My daughter had one abortion, which she says was relatively painless, legal and modestly priced. She has had two children since. In addition to her manic-depression, she had gestational diabetes. She was sterilized during the last cesarean section. She has never regretted any of it. She is now severely diabetic and prays that she will live long enough to raise her girls.

It must be remembered that this struggle is not about theology, it is not about ideology, it is not even about biology. _It is about power._ If we lose, God help us all.

Abortion: In A Word

abortion
choice

pain
bleeding

decision
empowerment

suction
sadness

grief
relief

cramping
crying
sighing

cannula
laminaria
forceps

fear
loss

joy
worry
womb

uterus
cervix
body
autonomy
control

conflict
politics
picketers

rights
restrictions
resolutions
RELIEF

women make the choice of abortion every day
elsewhere in the world

where abortion is illegal
women die

we must keep women safe

the pope calls abortion "the shame of humanity"
what happened to
poverty
war
hunger
racism
ethnic genocide
maldistribution of resources

why do women choose abortion?
they choose it for themselves
for their families
they choose it for survival

I fear the knitting needle
the coat hanger
I fear we are going back
politicians try to restrict abortion
imposing their morality
this leads to such tragedy

I cry for the baby abandoned in a dumpster
what pain and desperation that mother must have felt
that poor child

abortion is a moral choice
an ethical choice
we must keep women safe
we must continue to speak out

the struggle continues

speak out for women
women's lives
women's choices
speak out for RESPECT

Abortion helps women become better mothers
when they are ready
only the woman can look within herself
and know the truth of what she must do
it is not simple or easy

I have never known life to be simple or easy
Have you?

— by Marcy L. Bloom

In my work in the 1970's with the agency dispensing medical coverage in California, many cases of necessary abortion came to my attention. I am violating no confidence by relating the following experience.

One case that stands out in my mind is one in which I did not see the child needing the abortion, since her family already had Medi-Cal. The school nurse called me to consult on the matter. She had learned that this 12 year old Laotian hill country child of a refugee family was pregnant. The nurse took her for an examination at a women's clinic, and the resulting conclusion was that the child was being frequently sexually abused by an adult in the family, or close to the family.

Can anyone really believe that this child in that family would have any chance in this world if saddled with an infant at the age of 12-13? And what chance is there for a child conceived of such a close relationship with continuing incestuous abuse (the most reasonable assumption)? There is little likelihood that the baby would have been given up for adoption with that ethnic background.

Who has the right to condemn a 12 year old to bear a child? Who has the right to condemn an infant to servitude in an incestuous family? Never to have been born is better than that life sentence.

To the American People

I am dismayed at the spate of recent "Pro Life" materials and programs that focus on the fate of the embryo. Can we deny the feelings and wishes of the women who face unwanted pregnancies?

As a women's health care nurse practitioner, I have assisted countless women who struggle with the decisions regarding unplanned/unwanted pregnancies.

The following three choices should always remain available:

1. To maintain the pregnancy and keep the child.

2. To maintain the pregnancy and relinquish the child for adoption.

3. To terminate the pregnancy via a safe, legal, and accessible abortion.

To limit the choices in any way causes the women involved to participate less fully in their own destinies.

Margaret Sanger once said, "Every child, a wanted child." As long as the existing contraceptive technology permits birth control failures to occur, the need for voluntary terminations of pregnancy will be forever with us. Anyone who can recall the horror of mangled bodies and deaths caused by illegal abortions or self-inflicted efforts to terminate pregnancies before the landmark Roe vs. Wade decision of 1973, must feel that return to those times would indeed be a step backward for our society.

Please support continued efforts at improving contraceptive technology. Until perfection in this area is achieved, please continue your support of a woman's right to choose a safe, legal abortion.

Its hard to tell a "story" about the most private, painful time in my life; but if one voice makes a difference, here is mine.

When I was 21, I was dating "the love of my life." Who knows the reason things work out the way they do, but I got pregnant. This was in 1970 before abortions were legal. When I told John I was pregnant, he said "As much as I like you, I don't love you enough to marry you." I'll probably never forget that one sentence. I had already decided to give the baby up for adoption if he didn't want to marry me. The reasons were many, but mostly I believed a child should have a mother and a father and I was terrified at the thought of raising a child alone. On February 11, 1971, I had a 6 lb. 10 oz. baby boy. Except for the few seconds after he was born, I never saw him. Its been 14 years since that year (or 9 months in my life) and though I don't regret the decision I made, sometimes the sadness and pain are just as great now as then.

People told me what a loving, unselfish, wonderful thing I had done, and how happy I'd made some childless couple. And I suppose that is all true. My heart still goes out to girls who give up their babies. For some, back before abortions were legal, giving up a baby was just a way to get rid of it; just as abortions are now for some. For some of us it was the saddest, most bitter and painful thing that ever happened.

In the spring of 1971, after I had given my baby up for adoption, Christ came into my life. He has been with me ever since. He is the one constant in my life and has given me a lot of strength and peace of mind. Life goes on and you can imagine my shock, horror and stupidity when in the spring of 1973, I discovered I was pregnant again. This time by a guy I had known for a few months and had just stopped dating. I was 23. The thing I knew from the first was that I couldn't go through giving another baby away. There would be no marriage this time either. And with being a Christian now, I knew abortion was against God. Things were a lot more complicated. It was a rough decision, but 8 weeks into

it, I had an abortion. I went into the hospital and had it done surgically. I didn't want to be awake or know what went on. I remember the first feeling I had when I woke up – relief! "I'm not pregnant anymore," I thought.

Maybe that feeling was God's way of telling me it was OK. Maybe because I talked to Him about it and prayed and said, "I'm sorry, forgive me, but I just can't give another baby away." Maybe that is why I've never had any guilt about my abortion. If I shed any tears now, as I have while I've written this, it's for my son that I'll never know.

Some of us will always have a pain we'll have to live with. Whether its a lost love, the child we'll never have, the abortion we had or didn't have. But one thing we all deserve to have is a choice – the right to decide ourselves.

I had a "legal" abortion in Washington state in 1966. In 1966 it was next to impossible to get a legal abortion. At the time I was a 23 year old mother of three pre-school age children, and I had been separated from my husband for about five weeks when a man broke into my house and raped me. I was awakened from my sleep because I couldn't breathe. He was pressing a wooden dowel against my windpipe and I blacked out. When I came to, he had a knife at my throat and he told me to keep quiet or he would kill me. At the time my then six month old son was sleeping in a crib about six feet away from my bed. The rapist also had a pillow over my face so that I couldn't see him. In the two minutes that it took him to do his crime of terror I was becoming increasingly aware of the 1,000 things he could do. Would he kill me and my three babies, what could I do to save us; if he didn't kill us how was I going to get help?

When he left I looked out from under the pillow to take a mental picture of him – he was so average looking, white, about 5'9", of slight build, about 28 years old – he could have been the proverbial man-next-door, he was some woman's man-next-door. I called the police, they came and eventually caught the slime bag. He had been on parole after doing 18 months on two previous rapes and had been out of prison just a few weeks. The police in Seattle in 1966 were men who believed rape was something sexual and they asked all of the ludicrous questions of me like did I talk to strangers, did I walk around outside in provocative clothing, and did I leave my curtains open when I was dressing? In other words, what did I do to cause this pathetic, abnormal man to want – no, need – to put his penis in me?

About three weeks later (and re-raped by the law enforcement officers), I started having morning sickness. I went to my Catholic male gynecologist who confirmed the further trauma – my body (myself) was still being invaded by the rapist's power game. I then tried to find out about getting an abortion. My gynecologist wouldn't even have me as a patient any more after I told him I was considering abor-

tion. My shrink said he believed I qualified for a legal abortion under the only provision – danger to the life of the mother – because I might die if I tried to abort myself, or if I went to the back-alley abortionist, but he couldn't be a witness in court because it went against his religious beliefs. He told my still-legal husband that he could have me committed (another common occurrence). Then when the rapist's child was delivered, my husband could sign the papers to have it put up for adoption. (In 1966 women were 300% more chattel than now. A psychiatrist could say he felt that proceeding with the pregnancy might cause death by suicide of the mother.)

I then called the police detective working on the case and asked if he could tell me how I could go about getting a "legal" abortion. He said I couldn't get a legal abortion and that if I did have an abortion they would throw me in jail and charge me with manslaughter. I told him he might end up throwing my corpse in jail.

I tried various means to self-abort. These were some of the traditional techniques that I learned from some of my women friends and acquaintances. It seemed like half of the women I knew then had pills, potions, catheter tubes and other aborting procedures and equipment. None of these worked. I only got a series of severe infections. I then started asking people I knew if they knew how to contact the back-alley abortionists. I got some names and addresses and with the help of my mother, began searching out the next possible solution to my trauma, but all of the butchers were out of town. I found out later it was because of the tolerance policies of Seattle and Portland. The abortionists were run out of Seattle while the prostitutes were being run out of Portland and they traded towns every six months.

After this fiasco I decided to talk to "legitimate" doctors and I called a doctor I had seen in the past. It turned out that he was the chairman of the board at Stevens Hospital and knew the laws. He told me what I would have to do to get a "legal" abortion. I had to go to University hospital and see the doctor who was the head of the in-patient depart-

ment of psychiatry. He told me that he, personally, saw no reason that I shouldn't be able to get an abortion, except of course, the law. He had just returned from working in Japan on some exchange program and he said that over there women went in and got abortions on request. Afterward, they could then go next door and have plastic surgery to repair their hymens. He coached me on how to "perform" for the three psychiatrists I would have to see in the outpatient department who, along with him, would meet with the hospital board and make their recommendation. I was trying to get it under the stipulation that the health of the mother was in jeopardy. This category broadly included mental health reasons. To get the abortion I had to "act" like a schizophrenic personality for one doctor (his favorite disorder), a catatonic depressive for another (witch) doctor, and anxiety depressive, suicidal for another. I got my "legal" abortion – I also got an education in the way the patriarchal system works. I had to deal with insensitive, ignorant cops, demented mental health "experts", tyrannical male-god worshippers, and the one man in this insanity who was given an appropriate label: the (main) rapist. They were all rapists. They all wanted to have control over me, they all wanted to "be on top."

This was when I began to seriously speculate on how widespread and all invasive this maniacal disease of female abuse is. I lost my blinders. I began to see men as the incomplete gender. I began to see that the emperor had no clothes, it was a pack of depraved boys posing as "authorities." Men as half people, as frightened lemmings, awestruck by their male god, believing the patriarchal myths, being overly impressed by their limited sexuality, their limited capacity to feel or know. I now see it as grown men trying to force their superstitions on everyone (they call it a religion of HIM worshipping). THE RAPIST – THE LAW ENFORCER – THE DOCTOR – I CONTENDED WITH THEIR UNHOLY TRINITY ... I won in my battle to have minimal control over my own life ... but it shouldn't have been that hard and I become furious when I hear self-righteous people trying to force that same kind of (in)justice on women today!!

In the late 20's and early 30's I worked as a Bacteriologist and a Biochemist in a certain medical clinic in Seattle. I saw some of our doctors try to save the lives of women who had become infected after abortions in "back-alleys."

Believe it or not one abortionist was a plumber who was written up in a newspaper later.

A few lives were saved – some were not.

Katharina's Story

Sitting across the table, Katharina looks up at me and sighs;
"Rach, you know, I don't know where to begin."
I take her hand and reply,
"You know, neither do I."

It was a chilly fall evening and I sat in a cafe with my close friend, Katharina, and wept as she recounted for me the painful experience of having an abortion several months earlier. It was a story she had, as of then, never told anyone in full nor allowed herself to remember. That previous summer, only weeks before we were all to return to college for our senior year, an unplanned and unwanted pregnancy left her with a difficult decision. Given circumstances of her life at the time, involved with a man she was not committed to, in addition to being almost finished with school, she chose to have a menstrual extraction, an early term abortion performed without complications by a local OB/GYN. While the actual procedure was legal, accessible and affordable, the experience was emotionally traumatic and left her struggling to reconcile seemingly contradictory feelings within the context of a highly politicized public debate about abortion. She was confused and alone, afraid to speak to anyone and unsure of what to say.

This is the product of a series of informal conversations with Katharina and an attempt to consolidate what struck me as some of her main fears when speaking about her abortion. I asked her open-ended questions in order to allow her concerns to shape the direction and structure of our discussions. Our friendship lent a sense of mutual trust, honesty and enthusiasm beneficial to any ethnographic endeavor. Our connection has held me accountable for my role as both researcher and friend, and pushed me to be especially aware of how my own assumptions about abortion played into our discussions.

Over the span of several months, I recognized two themes arising from my discussions with Katharina. The first was her memories of the actual procedure, namely her interaction with various medical personnel. The second was her struggle to reconcile her feelings of shame and loss with an adamant pro-choice position. In turn, I find these two issues to powerfully inform and reinforce one another.

The doctor, he was horrible, the therapist at Planned Parenthood warned me about him. I was desperate. He was so cold, unfeeling, and did not let my mom come in with me. "Relax your muscles," as if they could relax on command! It was as if I were here to get my teeth pulled. I was petrified, shaking. I was so trusting that they would know how to take care of me, it was so disturbing — who knows my body better than me? He asks me to relax without asking why the muscles were tense in the first place ... He was in a rush, had more appointments that day. It hurt, more painful because my muscles were cramped. He wouldn't explain anything to me, just said I'd have cramps. I'd never had cramps before. This scary hand was touching my body, he had big, fat fingers, I didn't know what was happening. After he left, I felt so sick. I just wanted my mom to come in, I was so tense — he said to get dressed but I couldn't move — I sensed I needed to leave, it wasn't my space. Someone else would be coming in, I had to get out of there. I was nauseous. I was so thirsty, I needed some water. I just wanted to connect with someone. I asked the nurse for water; she, too, was so unfeeling. I felt totally alone. The doctor had no qualms about performing the menstrual extraction, he just couldn't relate to me as a human being .... The nurse saw my blood staining the paper, she ripped it off and put a clean piece on the table, all ready for the next woman. They didn't relate to me as a human being ...

Katharina's abortion was legal, safe and performed by a doctor renowned for technical competency, yet nonetheless her recollection is wrought with fear and discomfort. She asserts that she knows her body better than anyone yet the doctor attempts to make her feel otherwise, not respecting her as a holistic human being. While privileged with the access to reproductive health services, Katharina's experience was controlled and shaped by the caprice of an insensitive abortion provider.

While able to direct anger at her insensitive care providers, the judgmental way in which she was treated lent to feelings of shame and guilt for having gone through with the procedure:

> *I felt kind of ashamed of the whole thing, that it had happened so fast. I felt like I took the easy way out, avoided judgment towards the responsibility of pregnancy. I erased it from public view. If I had gone to the same doctor with a sore throat he wouldn't have judged me .... I feel so strongly about women having the right to choose yet I feel so ashamed ....*

Luckily, Katharina had the chance to speak with a counselor at a feminist health clinic prior to having the abortion. In listening to Katharina recount her meeting with this woman, I was incredibly moved by the support she was offered at this critical time, helping her to place the situation in a larger context and affirm her right to make decisions that fit with her life circumstances.

> *She* [the therapist] *told me that abortion does not equal negation, that it is dealing with a circumstance in a practical way ... I was so profoundly influenced by the people around me, I was so vulnerable to what everyone thought, I needed support. What she said made me feel better, and stayed with me. I'm so thankful for her underlying support, I'm so frightened for people who don't have that. She said it was important to see myself not as*

a product of a pregnancy, but as a whole person — that being pregnant doesn't fundamentally define who I am. She tries to learn as much about people as she can, each woman has a unique story, there are cultural stigmas attached to abortion. It makes it hard to make decisions based on what is good for us, what fits into our lives. What do I need? Where does this pregnancy fit into my life?

The solace Katharina found in this holistic, concrete perspective was countered by the pressure to compartmentalize her feelings and deny the contradictions embedded in her response to a complex situation.

Abortion is such a platform issue — I don't know how I felt, couldn't say what I felt was right for me — couldn't separate myself from the cultural debate and politicized rhetoric. This hindered me from trusting my feelings. I felt trapped inside of what I thought I should do rather than what I felt inside. I feel so strongly about women having the right to choose and yet I feel so ashamed ....

Feeling "trapped" indicates to me how serious an impact the pressure from all sides of the abortion debate had on Katharina's decision-making process, obscuring her own feelings and needs at this particular moment in time. When I asked Katharina to elaborate on why she felt so ashamed, she turned to the notion of motherly instincts and a fear that having an abortion defied her own desire and/or ability to care for a child.

I have motherly instincts, I want to be a mother. I feel like the abortion went against that instinct ... this experience forced me to pit my mothering instincts against the specific circumstances I was under. It was an internal tug-of war, part of me felt this was natural and part was telling me this was not what I wanted right now.

The abortion felt like a rejection yet I couldn't deal with being a mother right then .... I don't want to have a child until I'm ready to do a good job, until I'm mature enough. I'm so self-absorbed right now. I don't think I can handle myself yet .... I have a history and a future and I can shape that future too. Maybe this happened because I needed to abort, perhaps pregnancy is not a prescribed path, maybe my "fate" was to talk to you, to learn through this, to work on this project with you. Who's to say what's natural? Jerry Falwell??

Katharina's questioning the viability of her own "motherly instinct" reveals how pervasive the Right's notion of abortion as morally problematic has become in the public consciousness. It is upsetting for me to hear the extent to which Katharina has internalized the rhetoric espoused by anti-abortion forces, particularly the myth that mothers do not have abortions. At the same time, however, Katharina's self-awareness and thoughtful reasoning about motherhood resist conservative ideology and assert her need to actively shape her own future.

Remembering her experience, Katharina remarks that:

I had access to the medical care, but the people were inaccessible, not understanding ... the nurse at the emergency room treated me like shit, judged me, blamed me. Everyone thought I was being so irresponsible ... just another pregnant teenager. I can still remember her looks, her words were so biting. I felt horrible ... she asked me all about the technical history, when the bleeding had started and so forth .... I don't know if they realize how big an impact their words, their actions had on my life, and I can only imagine how many other women felt that too ....

This statement reminds me how important it is to fight for more than just legal access to abortion services, but for medical care that supports and affirms women's choices,

taking into account our social and political context. By not challenging our health care providers, we sanction their moral authority and "professional" control over our bodies.

I don't enjoy the thought of having let go of a potential child ... but it's about my need to set my own agenda, say when I'm ready to have a child and with whom ... no one has the right to put claim on my uterus, my reproductive organs ... why don't they go around arresting men for erections in public! Why don't they put legislation on this?

Katharina's comment frames opposition to abortion accessibility in terms of women's subjugation in a patriarchal society. Katharina's feelings of isolation in her struggle to reconcile her emotional response with a political "pro-choice" conviction illuminates the failure of the single issue abortion rights movement to embrace the full, circumstantial reality of women's lived experience. The emotional and spiritual responses to an aborted pregnancy need not contradict a movement for abortion rights, but can rather lead us to a more holistic vision of women's health and liberation.

I feel frustrated that I didn't think of all this before. I was so unprepared for the idea of being pregnant and needing to abort .... I want other women to feel more prepared, I want to be a resource. We can all be authorities ... this could happen to anyone, we therefore need to talk about it, prepare ourselves, talk about the contradictions. We need to recognize, validate our own particular circumstances and remember that things we do are OK.

Legalized and accessible abortion for all women is only a beginning. I see universal health insurance and women-controlled reproductive health care as crucial goals of a com-

prehensive women's health movement. While our personal responses to abortion may be difficult to reconcile, by remaining committed to a vision for progressive social transformation, we can collectively fight against all forms of oppression and exploitation.

Excerpted from a paper by Rachel Perlmutter
Oberlin College, 1997
Rachel is currently the Office Manager at
Aradia Women's Health Center, Seattle, WA

In discussing abortion once with my mother, a 70-year resident of Wenatchee, she told me that when she was in her 40's she had quite a bit of back trouble. My dad thought a chiropractor would be a good idea (this was the 1940's in Wenatchee, WA). There was one practicing 2-3 miles away who was supposedly good, but Mom said he also practiced abortion on the side. When Mother went to have her back adjusted, there were little booths with white curtains in front for patients to undress in - she heard the nurse come by and say "No, not her, she's here for her back!"

With ANIMALS and their biology, when hormones say MATE they mate! HUMANS have options.

Although our sexuality is also regulated by hormones ... by our own free will, by values, opportunity, inhibitions, adult examples, values and education, it can be swayed by many outside (and internal) factors.

Inhibitions can be swayed by the media, and numerous events, feelings and substances as in, "A few drinks and a one-night-stand"... or another familiar phrase, "get lucky."

Our sexuality responses can also be swayed by peer pressure and a teen's home environment. So many things can enter into a spontaneous teen decision.

If the woman becomes pregnant by any of the above reasons, by incest, rape, or other instances of force, there may be a "shot-gun wedding."

Romance? A WANTED child? A PLANNED child? Seldom does this work out. Kids having kids is a tragedy waiting to happen.

Most are an "OOPS"... and not planned!!

In the most extreme case, consider a woman who becomes pregnant and gives birth every year, yes EVERY YEAR of her fertile life. It is theoretically possible for her to have 35 children.

In this SAME period, if a man had unprotected sexual intercourse just ONCE a week he could father 1,820 children. Add his increased years of fertility (many into their 80's and 90's), and his potential for physical domination over women the number of uncontrolled sperm can impregnate hundreds, even thousands of individual women.

ONE egg (each month) vs. 20, 000,000 sperm (each normal ejaculation) ... DUHHHHH!

We have been sold a story ... a myth ... we have been brainwashed to believe in "happily-ever-after" ... while even adults who marry do not have relationship skills such as anger-management, conflict-resolution or parenting skills.

ALL of life is a trade-off. When we say YES to something, we also say NO to something else.

— Bette Gall-Vaughn

Close to ten years ago I had one of the purest experiences in making a decision which would impact my future in a way possibly no other decision might influence my life. I was 20 years old and my IUD had failed in its job to prevent my becoming pregnant.

My decision was not difficult. I pictured my life, my future as a single parent, seeking public assistance, medical coupons, delaying my degree, quitting my job.

But the most significant factor in my decision was anticipating giving birth to a child I did not want. I was not prepared either economically or emotionally, and I recognized that this child would surely know the impact s/he had made on my life and happiness.

Having been raised in a family with the knowledge that I was an "accident," and "was not expected," and possibly ruined my parents' relationship and their individual lives was knowledge enough for me. I resolved that I would try — never to do such a thing to a child of my own.

So, it was a simple, clear-minded, and *personal* decision to have an abortion. A decision based on my own individual experience and circumstances at the time. I have never regretted this decision.

I had an illegal abortion in the early 1950's. Then, I was a young lieutenant in the regular army. The man by whom I became pregnant was also a career officer. Then, the IUD and the pill were not available, and a military gynecologist refused to prescribe a diaphragm for me because I was unmarried. At that time, if I had been married, I could not have gotten into the army for the training I wanted. I could not remain on active duty while pregnant, nor could I stay in the military with a child. Additionally, I could not get an abortion in the army hospital to which I was assigned. Thank God times have changed!

I had my pregnancy confirmed by a civilian gynecologist. He thought that I should resign my commission and have the baby. However, he lost interest when I said that there was no way I could get a loan to pay him for prenatal care and delivery unless I had a job. Getting any civilian employment, much less work in my profession, would be next to impossible under the circumstances. I assured him that my parents not only would not help me out financially, but also would disown me if they knew I was pregnant. My lover, using the time-worn male cop-out of "How do I know it's mine?" absolved himself of all responsibility financial and otherwise. Furthermore, I did not want to get out of the army.

I was well into the second trimester before a friend in a distant city located an unlicensed M. D. to perform the abortion. It cost me $800 plus plane fare. Then, I earned about $225 per month. Following surgery, I hemorrhaged for two days, unable to contact the vanished abortionist and afraid to contact legitimate medical help.

Malicious gossip by women officers twenty years my senior about my suspected pregnancy reached my hospital commander and I was called into his office. However, by the time that happened, I had undergone the abortion and could answer honestly, when challenged, that I was not pregnant. When asked if I had been pregnant, I told him that it was none of his business. I was reprimanded for immorality

and insolence and transferred to another duty station. That reprimand remained in my official records for years and caused me to be passed over for a promotion, special schooling, and choice assignments. However, the episode did establish my reputation as a heterosexual in the military community so that I was spared the harassment of the army's witch hunts for lesbians.

Thirty years later I feel that I made the right choice in having an illegal abortion. I was able to pursue a useful and rewarding career in the service of my country. That would not have been possible if I had born a child. Better the "silent scream" of an aborted fetus than the audible anguish of an unwanted child and an unwilling mother. I feel now as I did then that abortion should be legal, available, and affordable; that it should be financed for poor women in this and third world countries with tax dollars; that it should be used to terminate any unwanted pregnancy, but should not be used as a preferred method of birth control. While I feel that abortion should be used to terminate unwanted pregnancies, it should be considered a private matter between a woman and her physician. Ranging from meddlesome to maudlin to terrorist, the tactics of those who oppose abortion intrude further into a woman's personal life than do the instruments of the abortionist. Because I do not care to again be challenged by people who presume to tell me how I should have lived my life, I remain anonymous.

Why I Believe in Pro Choice

Ever since I overheard some of my mother's friends quietly discussing what one among them could do to terminate an unwanted pregnancy, I've been concerned about a woman's inability to have control over her own body. I was about ten years old at the time-and the sense of concerned empathy expressed by these middle-class, small-town women in their late thirties stayed with me for the next fifty years. When the right of choice to an abortion became the law of the land I felt relieved — no more "abortion mills", self-imposed ruinous attempts, "back-alley" unsanitary, uncaring procedures, or safe choices for those with money.

And now — ten years later — there are those who would again leave a woman with no safe choice.

I am now 71 years old and I'm crying out — WE CAN'T GO BACK!!!

My life had been so skewed and harmed by my illegal abortion that I feel very strongly abortion should remain legal.

In 1960 I was living in Wisconsin with my boyfriend, on whom I depended very greatly for emotional security. He was married but separated, and had one small child who lived with us. When I got pregnant in spite of my using a diaphragm, he said he would leave me unless I had an abortion.

It's probably hard for most women today to understand the great sense of dependence of women upon men for their own sense of identity. Twenty-five years ago, in my case, the idea of being abandoned and pregnant was too shameful to accept. I was horrified at the thought of having an illegitimate child, and of dropping out of college to have it. Shame was my main response.

So I let my boyfriend find a contact (an Italian Catholic with six children who claimed Mafia connections, in fact). This person knew an abortionist in another town (an aging and trembling surgeon, later convicted when a girl died), and we rustled up the $700 (1960 dollars) by borrowing from friends. I squirmed on that cold steel table as he probed and scraped without anesthetic.

About a week later I began having abdominal pains and a fever. I was working as a typist to pay back the money. I felt like a murderer. There wasn't any counseling then. I kept on sitting and typing for several more weeks as the pains got worse and worse. Finally I nearly fainted and people were telling me I was white as a sheet. I figured I deserved it for killing the child. I figured I needed punishing. At last I figured I would die if I didn't go to a doctor. I was terrified because I expected the doctor to tell the police. I was caught between two fears, but the fear of dying won. My problem turned out to be endometriosis, the likely result of having my uterus punctured. Nine months after getting pregnant, I had a hysterectomy. I was 21. I told myself that in the future all I would ever produce would be shit.

A while later my boyfriend and I got married, life rocked along for a while. I got one degree, then another, his daughter was still living with us. I wanted to adopt a child or two, but he didn't want to. Much later he left me, telling me he wanted more children and this other woman wasn't sterile. I was devastated. It took about three years to get angry.

This is rather a cold recital because I am still angry about all of this. Girls should be raised to depend upon themselves and take care of themselves. No one should do it for them or should be able to make the kind of decision that I let someone else make on my behalf. Women should have choices regarding their bodies and should make those choices for themselves. No man or governmental body of men should make those choices for women. *Ever.*

Killing in the Name of Life?

He approached with his menacing steely blue eyes. Over six feet tall with blond hair and talking non-stop, he seemed somewhat disturbed. As we entered the hotel he told us that God's word had been revealed to him and that God would punish all of us someday soon. It was a strange and frightening scene.

The place was Pensacola, Florida. The occasion was the memorial anniversary for David Gunn, M.D. Dr. Gunn, who traveled to provide abortions to women in under-served areas in Florida, Georgia, and Alabama, had been assassinated the year before by an anti-choice terrorist. One year later, on March 13, 1994, women's clinic personnel from throughout the country had come together to remember and to honor our fallen colleague.

When we arrived at the Pensacola Grand Hotel, and also the next day at the memorial site of Dr. Gunn's tragic murder, Paul Hill was present. Again, he was loud, intimidating, and his glazed blue eyes were filled with hatred and loathing. Hill held signs stating "Dr. Gunn Deserved to Die" and "Don't Mourn Baby Killers, Mourn Dead Babies." He and other members of "Defensive Action" — the organization of which Hill is director — spoke to the media, stating that homicide was justifiable against abortion clinic staff. Hill compared abortion to the Nazi holocaust and abortion providers to Adolf Hitler. "They deserve anything that happens to them," Hill said to a reporter. The group advocated freedom for Michael Griffin, Dr. Gunn's assassin, in the name of "justifiable homicide."

The memorial for Dr. Gunn was both comforting and disturbing. It was comforting to learn more about the life of this kind and dedicated physician, and disturbing to see the hate and contempt in the eyes of Paul Hill and his cohorts as they raged that a man deserved to die. As is true for much of the anti-choice terrorist behavior, it is absolutely incomprehensible.

Confronting and coping with anti-choice militants and terrorists is not new to those of us who work and advocate for compassionate women's health services. But when I heard Paul Hill shouting that women who had chosen abortion also deserved to die because they had killed their babies, I was terrified. In the name of God and a fundamentalist interpretation of the Bible, these people espoused killing in the name of life. I knew this twisted and perverted hatred could only lead to more tragedy, violence, and pain.

Four months later, on Friday morning, July 29th, 1994, it led to the murders of John Britton, M.D., 69, and his volunteer escort, James Barrett, 74. Barrett's wife, June, 68, was wounded, but will make a full physical recovery. Hill was caught running away, still carrying the murder weapon — a 12-gauge shotgun. He was charged with two counts of premeditated murder and one count of attempted murder, and today, a convicted murderer, he sits on Florida's death row as his appeal continues.

Hill is not able to hurt any of us anymore, but what remained was the fear and concern over who will be next. Amazingly, the "next" occurred only a few months later in Brookline, Mass., on Dec. 30, 1994, when Shannon Lowney and Leanne Nichols were murdered at two women's clinics by a lone gunman named John Salvi, who later drove hundreds of miles and shot out the windows at a clinic in Virginia. What could possibly drive these individuals to such insane acts?

Killing in the name of life is a concept that has no justification, except to the deranged and disturbed religious fanatic. Yet for more than twenty-five years women's health clinics have endured protests, pickets, blockades, threats, harassment, stalkings, arsons, bombings , and now three valuable people are dead. Still, even with all this terrifying violence, women continue to have abortions. On the day of those murders, abortions continued at Aradia Women's Health Center. Our clients could tell that we were somewhat jittery, and we told them why, in quiet, relaxing tones. No one left. Even when we received a death threat six days

later, we went on with our work. That is, after all, why we,
as a non-profit women's health center, have existed for
twenty-five years. Aradia Women's Health Center exists to
offer women respect, choices, education, and information as
women actively participate in their health care.

More than 1.5 million women make the choice of
abortion each year in the U.S. alone. An estimated 25 million abortions are performed annually throughout the world.
Women make this choice because they cannot have a baby at
a particular time in their lives. They make this choice because relationships are imperfect, promises are broken, contraception fails, and because sexuality and sexual activity are
still confusing and veiled topics in our society. Women
choose abortion because the achieving of many of life's
dreams and goals are often painful and difficult; because
health problems and personal crises occur; and because raising a child in today's world — whether married or single —
is increasingly frightening and complex. Women choose
abortion because they need to survive.

Yet the stigma of abortion remains. Women still whisper the word abortion when they call for an appointment,
or for information about our care. Some women still fear
that something bad will happen to them when they make
this choice ...."Will God punish me?" We reassure women
that God is loving, and understands why we often must make
tough and difficult choices in our lives.

All of us who believe in a woman's right to reproductive health care and the importance of all women's health
services must continue to speak out and acknowledge abortion as a moral choice — just as valid and ethical as the choice
of having a baby. Women are ethical and moral decision-
makers and need support, compassion and respect, not violence, no matter what choice they make when faced with an
unplanned pregnancy. Only by speaking out clearly and
passionately against the stigma of abortion and the
marginalization of abortion services — and by validating
the realities of women's lives — can women choosing abortion and those of us who provide women's health care begin

99

to feel that perhaps another tragedy against an abortion provider is not imminent.

The revulsion we all experienced when we recognized that three deaths had occurred at the hands of anti-choice militants must now be channeled into positive community action and support. All pro-choice men and women must ensure that their own communities, their own clinics, and their own physicians and clinic staff are not targeted for intimidation and violence.

I recently learned that a good friend of mine, the administrator of Everywoman's Health Centre in Vancouver, British Columbia, was assaulted by an anti-choice militant echoing the views of Paul Hill. Meanwhile, amidst anti-abortion rights hecklers, a memorial service was being held on August 3rd for Dr. John Britton in his hometown of Fernandina Beach, Florida. Inside the church, he was remembered and honored as a compassionate and committed physician. And tragically — just as at Dr. Gunn's memorial — an anti-choice militant demonstrated outside yelling "Britton deserved to die." He brandished an award with the inscription: "Marksmanship Trophy for God's Hero Brother Hill."

When will the hatred end?

I wonder: will there be another Pensacola ... ? another Brookline ... ? somewhere ... ?

Marcy L. Bloom is the Executive Director of Aradia Women's Health Center in Seattle. She has worked in the field of women's health services, abortion care, and reproductive rights activism since 1968.

Woody's Story

A typical beginning and an almost tragic ending, it was 1967 and Woody got pregnant thinking her boyfriend would marry her. Of course, that didn't happen. She was only 21and had lost her mother a year or two before. Her father had recently remarried and Woody did not know her new stepmother or stepsisters very well. She desperately needed to tell her father, but didn't want to shame him in front of his new family so she kept her bad news to herself.

Not only did her boyfriend not marry her, he did not even help her find a reliable person to perform the abortion or contribute any help for the event. Woody got a name from an "experienced" girl at the office and made all the arrangements herself. She met the abortionist at a cheap motel and before performing the abortion he suggested they "get it on" seeing as how she was already pregnant.

Woody was sickened by the suggestion and, thank God, the abortionist left her alone. After the abortion Woody returned to her apartment, alone. Sometime later, she started bleeding severely. She managed to contact a neighbor who got her to a hospital. Fortunately, she survived.

No woman should ever have to be subjected to the kind of personal anguish and indignity that Woody suffered. Clean, professional abortion clinics should be available for all women who seek such help.

"Given the same set of circumstances, I would take the same action."

— Unidentified woman who has had an abortion

As a medical social worker, I have worked with many families profoundly affected by unplanned pregnancies and the difficult decisions those pregnancies require. Let me tell you about two of those families.

When Susan came to the Medical Center where I worked, she was 31, the wife of a prosperous farmer, mother of two girls, 9 and 7, and happy to be 7 weeks pregnant. In the course of her prenatal work-up, Hodgkins' disease was discovered. The disease -- a potentially curable cancer -- was in its early stages but required immediate treatment which would seriously damage the fetus. Susan and her family weighed the alternatives -- carrying the pregnancy to term and delaying treatment while the Hodgkins' disease progressed past the point of possible cure or terminating the pregnancy and taking treatment immediately. Susan and her family chose abortion. It was not an easy decision for them but now, nine years later, Susan is disease-free and her daughters have had a mother when they most needed her.

When Joanne came to the Medical Center, she was 23, married to an unemployed roofer, mother of a three year old boy with speech and hearing problems and a five year old boy with hyperactivity. She had been referred to us for treatment of thyroid cancer. There was a great deal of love in Joanne's family but their multiple problems forced them to survive from one day to the next knowing that any additional stress could be the last straw. Joanne's chemotherapy and radiation made her menstrual periods irregular so her pregnancy was not diagnosed until about 12 weeks. Joanne's alternatives were similar to Susan's - abortion with continued treatment for the cancer or discontinuing the treatment and carrying the pregnancy to term. But in Joanne's situation, there was the added consideration of almost certain damage to the fetus from radiation and chemotherapy. Joanne and her husband chose abortion. In the six years since then, her cancer has been in and out of remission and the family still functions from day to day but Joanne is alive.

The decisions these families made were not easy — they never are — but, had abortion not been available to them. Susan's daughters surely would not have their mother alive, and the delicate balance in Joanne's family would have collapsed under the weight of a handicapped infant and a dying mother. These are not as some would suggest, lives destroyed by abortion. They are, in the most *literal* sense, lives saved and families preserved by abortion.

Yes, it's time to tell our stories. I'm not quite able to be public with mine, but just writing it will be easy and I want to if it will help keep abortion available. I am 47, a college graduate, working and living in Everett with my family.

Back-alley abortion was the only choice in 1964 in Washington, D. C. I was single, 26, and pregnant. I know it happened on the horrible and emotional day that John F. Kennedy was shot. We had been in love for three years and could have married but we both realized that would have only been a second mistake, on top of our first mistake. So abortion seemed to be our only solution. All during the end of December we agonized about how and where to arrange it. We didn't have anywhere to turn for help. We were under terrible pressure every day to come up with an answer. The whole period was a nightmare for me.

In desperation, we thought of a friend who might have connections with someone who could help. Finally, with enormous relief we set up a date to meet with a woman (a prostitute and a lesbian!), who took me to the abortionist. I was about 8 weeks pregnant. She drove me alone into D. C. to a large red brick apartment building. In the third floor apartment two black women were sitting at a table drinking coffee. I gave them the envelope with $1200. A black man finally arrived carrying a satchel. With no preliminaries, he led me to a bare bedroom and began. He told me it would hurt and he would try to be very careful. He kept scraping and dropping bits of bloody tissue into a metal bucket. The pain was so intense and seemed to go on and on. I really don't remember feeling any emotion then. I suppose the relief of solving the problem was greater than my embarrassment and pain. At the end, he made me look into the bucket to prove he'd cleaned me out. He also gave me a white pill for infection.

I have never told anyone else about this abortion. But I have never had the slightest guilt about doing it. It was the only answer for us at that time. I had little idea of the dan-

gers to me from an abortion. There was no one to tell me. I believe that later, when I married, and was unable to get pregnant, that it was because my fallopian tubes were scarred closed due to infection from the unsterile abortion.

It didn't have to end that way, of course. If legal, safe abortions were available, none of this would have happened. If effective birth control methods had been available to me – a single woman – even the pregnancy could have been avoided.

It was a terrible, fearful situation to live through and I hope this letter will help keep some other woman from experiencing it as I did.

I lost my virginity at age 18.
I had an abortion at age 21.
Both experiences came too soon.
Emotionally and physically.

It's so very easy to make love.
Even easier to make babies.
I know now that love can be temporary.
And babies are forever.
And should be.

I never want to have another abortion.
I am now 24.
My child would have been 3 years old.
My child would have been in nursery school before I had
even finished college.

That baby would have been crying for love and attention
before I had even learned what love was.

I have since graduated from college.
I have a good job.
I am smarter now about contraception.
I wasn't smart then.
No one ever bothered to tell me how easy it was to make
a baby.
Making love and making babies are two very different things.
I know that now.

A lot of people make mistakes.
Getting pregnant at 21 was one of my biggest.
But I learned from that mistake, rather than being chained
to it, rather than resenting it ....

Because I had an abortion
My life is very different from what it could have been.
I made a choice when I decided not to have that baby.
A choice that I felt was right, and good, and necessary.
I know that I was one of the lucky ones,
lucky because I had a "choice."

The pain of my abortion is still with me.
I assume it always will be.
Choices often hurt.
I am glad that the baby I chose not to have is not hurting
because of my mistake.

The pain of a baby without love, and with a mother
unprepared and unwilling is the ultimate mistake;
the ultimate tragedy.
It wouldn't have been fair to me; more importantly,
    it would not have been fair to the baby.

(My story is the story of many thousands of women.
            For that reason, I prefer to remain anonymous.)
                                            May — 1985

In 1968 when I first moved to New York and before I found a permanent place to live or a job, my boyfriend from home came to visit me for a week. I was 23 at the time and abortion was illegal.

After about a month, I was pretty sure that I was pregnant. I called my boyfriend and asked him what he wanted me to do. He was an orphan and did not want to have any children. I did not want to have a child at that time and under those circumstances.

I went to a doctor to make sure I was pregnant. On the second visit he confirmed it. I asked him if he or anyone he knew could give me an abortion. He said no, but since I was already pregnant, would I have intercourse with him? I left his office in disgust.

Through people that I knew in the peace movement, I got the name of a man who could help me. I called this person and he told me that he worked with a group of doctors who performed abortions in the Bronx. The fee, which was $500, was going to be used for lobbying efforts to change the law against abortion. This man picked me up in his car on a pre-arranged street corner. I got in the car and we picked up another woman on the way. When we got to the Bronx, we went into an apartment building and into an apartment that had been converted into a doctor's office. I sat with a few other women in the living room while awaiting my turn. We shared our feelings.

The abortion itself was pretty painful. They couldn't use any strong pain medication due to the fact that we might have to leave quickly if the police came. After the abortion, the same man took me back to the street corner where he had picked me up. There was no aftercare, but I was given a mimeographed sheet which explained what types of problems that could arise and what to do about them.

I believe that my decision to have an abortion was a wise one. I'm glad that abortion is legal so that other women can make this type of personal choice without endangering their lives.

CHOICES

I was 23 years old in 1970. I was just leaving my husband of two years because I wanted more out of life than I was getting in that relationship. I suddenly found myself pregnant.

I felt I had four **choices**:

Go back to my husband to save face, though he was not the father.

Go home to my mother.

Become a single parent and try to make it on the $400 a month I made working.

Terminate my pregnancy.

My choice was number four. Abortion was illegal in Washington state at that time. There was a well-known doctor, however, who gave illegal abortions. He would be picked up and put in jail and would be back practicing within 30 days. He died in 1972.

I was happy when the law changed in 1973 to allow women that option legally. Women who felt they were trapped in a situation and may not be ready for the responsibility of a family. Even though it is legal, most women feel cheap even today for considering having an abortion.

Today I am 38 years old and I have not had to make that decision again. I believe that I became a more responsible person. This is my tenth year in my second marriage, and my husband and I have decided not to have children. I have a career where I manage two offices and ten employees.

Two weeks ago, one of my employees came to me crying. She said she just found out that she was pregnant. She said she felt trapped and all she wanted to do was "jump off a bridge." She is 23 years old, just celebrated her second wedding anniversary, and has a seven month old baby boy. She and her husband are having marital problems and she has considered leaving him several times. He is not working presently and her income is needed to support her family.

111

When she came to me I felt that I should offer her advice. I couldn't do that but I told her to remember that she did have a **choice**. Because of my experience I was able to comfort her and offer her some insights into the reality of abortion and the potential future problems.

She was frightened, depressed and physically ill just thinking about the options. She did think about her **choices**. She thought about the baby she has and the fact that she most likely will be a single parent within the next few years. She also thought about her earning capacity in relation to raising one or two children. She **chose** to terminate her pregnancy and work harder to put her marriage back together. She went to her *own* personal physician. He explained her options in medical terms and asked her to think carefully about what she wanted to do. When she finally came to a **choice**, he was very supportive and arranged to have the surgery in a local hospital.

I offered to take her to the hospital and the use my apartment for the rest of the day. Her surgery was scheduled for 8:30 a.m. but she had to be at the hospital by 6:30 a.m. to pre-register. She then had to wait for 2 hours before they took her into surgery. She was a bundle of nerves and I had to calm her down several times. She was scared and felt very much alone. Being legal doesn't always help but it's a start. The operation only took 15 minutes, but once again she had two hours to wait before she could leave. I took her to my place and she slept until 5:30 p.m., when she left to go home. She said she was feeling better already and feels that she has a new start with her family.

Her story is different from mine but she did have a **choice** and it was *legal*. I did not like having an abortion and neither did she. I don't know anyone who does. It is nice to know, however, that I have a **choice** to determine what happens to my own body.

I have a new outlook now, thanks to my friend's confidence in me. One thing she said, which I think is impor-

tant to mention, is that the word abortion should be changed to "termination of pregnancy". That sounds so much more appropriate.

I will continue to support Planned Parenthood and NARAL in the struggle to keep **choices** available for all women.

Dear NARAL

I am writing in support of abortion rights. I am pro-choice for several reasons. One is extremely personal; I chose to have an abortion years ago. I did not make the decision lightly; I do not view abortion as an "easy" alternative to birth control. I was unmarried, finishing up graduate school, not emotionally ready to be a mother/single parent and feeling irresponsible for not having taken better birth control measures. I would have gone to any lengths to have had the abortion and was glad there was a clinic in my city where I could receive legal and safe treatment. I feel very strongly that women should have such resources as well as positive information about their sexuality and effective birth control information. I also think men need to be more responsible in birth control measures, but not by forming policy that limits women's choices.

Another reason I am pro-choice is that I think our resources are finite, and we need to exercise control in our growth today in order to have a tomorrow for our youngsters. Also, I have been professionally involved with youth in need of adult affection and attention, yet programs that would provide that — such as Big Brother — usually do not have enough adult volunteers. I think of those programs and of the older and handicapped kids who wait to be adopted, when I hear of the arguments about childless couples "going without" while child-bearing women have abortions. There are so many ways to love children in this society, yet I've not seen an excess of love for the ones already here.

In closing, I would like to again voice my support for maintaining a woman's right to a safe and legal abortion.

— One Who Still Chooses
To Remain Anonymous

A Gift to a Stranger

Your words came at first
Slowly
Quietly
Tentative
You will cry
I thought
A wisp of hair brushed back
Were those tears I saw?
Your voice trembled – it will break!
I thought
Will you break?

I heard your fear
I sensed your anger
But then I felt your power
Calm
Certain
Determined
Focused
And the presence of others
Through your words you fed your quiet strength and
resolve
To them
And to me
The sum now greater than the parts
The whole complete in the one
In you
I am ashamed
I am not as strong as you
How can you be so strong?
But I know that answer
I had just forgotten for a while
One who chooses to be washed by the truth of the human
condition
Fear by one
Despair by another

Anger and betrayal by some
Anguished bitter choice by most
Nothing simple
Nothing easy
Nothing clear
Except
All alone and
All powerless to shift that choice to another

One who chooses to be washed by these waves
Must be a rock
In time that rock will be ground to sand
But many rocks
In time
Become a beach
Softening the blows of those waves
And joining mother earth with daughter sea
Those hollow creatures who cannot bear to look upon the
waves
They turn their eyes away
They refuse to feel the cold spray upon their faces
Their frenzied tongues shout
"Remove the rock and the waves will go away!"
And the rock is removed
And the waves do not go away
"Destroy the rock and the waves will go away!" they cry
And the rock is destroyed
And the waves do not go away
"Destroy the waves!" they scream
But they are cowards
They are afraid to stand upon your beach
And feel the pounding of those waves at their feet
They are afraid to feel the stinging spray upon their faces
They know they would be consumed by the truth of those
waves
Crushed and washed away without a trace remaining
They cower in their shelters

There is not a rock among them
Like you
And the waves continue

And your words continue
I feel jumbled emotions
Disbelief of your personal terror
Acceptance of its truth
Wonder at your inner beauty and strength
Anger at those who would harm you
Awe at your special agony
A woman's agony
Feeling much
Sharing some
Understanding little
Now I am suddenly alone
Wondering if I belong in such noble company
Then I feel joy and sorrow
Joy to share this moment in time with you and the others
Sorrow at the price you had to pay
That we all might have to pay
To be rocks

And in this all you have given me a gift
I struggle now
I try to clothe my emotions in words you can understand
I reach out to you with these words
Let them touch you when you are lonely
Let them caress you when you are fearful
And let them thank you for your gift to a stranger
You have returned to me the voice of my muted soul.

September 1984

*For B. W., who suffered the harassment and fire-bombing of her
Feminist Women's Health Center. And further dedicated to all
people who work on the cutting edge of women's rights.*

Taken from *Hear Me, White Man!* by Douglas Ragland

119

I recall being at college in Pullman from 1962 to 1966, and hearing girls whisper in the hallways of living areas or in our rooms that you could get an abortion on a "certain street" in Colfax. They also said there was a doctor who did them somewhere in the Smith Tower if you came to Seattle.

When I arrived in Seattle in 1967 I was able to see a gynecologist who has been my choice ever since, Richard Soderstrom. At the time, Dick was practicing at Virginia Mason Clinic. He readily gave out birth control pills if you were interested, and he was referring some abortion patients to Dr. Koome in Renton. I recall him speaking of two cases — one was a pregnant girl of 15 — the parents decided that she had to have the baby to "teach her a lesson." The second was a married woman who passed on a very debilitating and fatal nervous system disease to her two children who would die in their 20's. This woman was taking the pill, but had a GP who thought it was "bad" for her. She had returned to the diaphragm and became pregnant. She was hysterical at the thought of another child who would suffer and become ill like the first two.

Dr. Soderstrom took her case to the Board of VM, which did not approve an abortion because the life of the mother was not in danger. His last resort was to send her on to Dr. Koome.

I am sure that Dick Soderstrom in his compassion helped many women avoid pregnancy.

In 1971, at the age of 14, I became pregnant. I was in the 9th grade and was, what I considered, a relatively knowledgeable adolescent regarding sex. The pregnancy was a shock to me, as well as to my parents and an embarrassment to my brothers and sister. News of my pregnancy would have destroyed my "reputation" and that of my family's. We were long-time members of a small rural community in Iowa.

My pregnancy was terminated in New York City (which had legalized abortion then) amid total secrecy. I cannot describe my emotional suffering nor the heartbreak to my parents during this nightmare. But it was less than I would have suffered if I had been forced to parent a child alone at 15 in a community which would have ostracized me and my child.

After I found out about the pregnancy and before plans were made for my abortion, I had considered suicide or inducing my own abortion (I had a knitting needle selected for the job). I felt these were my only options under the circumstances. I have never regretted my decision to have the abortion. It was completed safely by trained physicians in a hospital.

I have, however, felt forsaken. I felt my church, my school, and my community had failed to protect me. None of these caretakers had provided me with the knowledge to protect myself against an unwanted pregnancy nor helped me sort through my values regarding my sexuality. Instead of providing me with much needed guidance, they left my sex education in the hands of the mass media. With the emphasis on the distortion of women's sexuality, it was not surprising that I became sexually active at such a young age. Everyone else was; I just got caught.

Because of the abortion I was able to finish school and continue on to graduate from college with honors. I am now the mother of a healthy, happy 10 month old daughter. I have a supportive husband and we both work. I pay taxes, actually making money for the country, not costing it money, as I would have if I had become a mother at 15.

Thirteen years have come to pass and I wish I could lay the whole experience to rest – but I can't. As long as men are determined to sentence young girls to the lifetime responsibility of motherhood for one innocent mistake and as long as the rights of all women to choose a safe and legal abortion are at risk, I'll continue reliving the nightmare, writing letters, and sending money in support of women's right to choose.

I was barely eighteen when I found myself pregnant and a sophomore in college. It was 1961; many years before legalized abortion. My parents and I agonized for what seemed an eternity and they decided, with my consent, that an abortion was the only alternative. It cost $200, a substantial amount in 1961, and it was illegal. Before I actually went to the abortionist, we drove to someone's home across the border in Pennsylvania (80 miles from my home in New York state) where that person prescribed straight gin and something else, which I can't remember, for a hoped-for miscarriage. It didn't work. My aunt and uncle became involved and they arranged for me to go to an abortionist in a nearby city (about 35 miles away). We drove there at night and met a driver who took me by myself to the home of the abortionist. He was *not* a doctor, I don't believe he ever studied medicine. He performed the abortion in an upstairs bedroom in his house using what I remember to be a rubber hose type apparatus. I vaguely remember being blindfolded so I couldn't see how we arrived at his house or how we returned to meet my aunt and uncle.

He told me that I would miscarry within the next 24-48 hours. What I believe actually happened was I lived through labor – it was the most excruciating pain I have ever experienced and it was without any pain medication or medical attention. He told me if I hemorrhaged, to say to the doctor at the emergency room that I had fallen on the ice and started to miscarry. Lucky for me I only fainted, and I did actually miscarry sometime during the next day.

I was scared; scared that something could go wrong; scared my now ex-boyfriend would find out; scared my friends would know. My biggest shame in 1961 was not the abortion but the fact that I had premarital sex and that made me a bad person. The abortion was my only choice. I chose to risk my life and break the law to save my future.

Please do whatever needs to be done to counteract the Pro-Life Movement. I don't believe any woman wants an abortion – it's always a monumental decision – but one we need to be allowed to make.

Fresh out of high school (1945), one of my classmates was 19 years old. She was the daughter of a coal miner's widow in a small town in Montana. She was pregnant, unwed and with very few, if any, options in those days. Afraid of the shame she'd bring her mother and family, she hanged herself.

A few years later my friend, whose husband was a student attending agriculture college in North Dakota, became pregnant. She opted for a kitchen abortion rather than have her husband leave college and start a family in hard economic times. She was found dead on the street.

In the late 50's in Kelso, WA, I heard about an abortion which was performed on a back street, in the back seat of a taxi. The instrument used for this procedure was a coat hanger. The young woman who had the abortion died as a result.

I am now 58 years old. I will always work and vote for the option of medically safe abortions for young women with unwanted pregnancies. I can't accept death as an option.

This letter is for my friend Gina. Gina, I am sure, would have written a letter for herself but she died in 1969. We were both freshman in college, 18 years old, full of adventure, and thought we knew everything. Gina died of septic shock caused by an infection from the illegal abortion she obtained in Mexico.

When Gina returned from Mexico, we knew she was sick, but she wouldn't go to the local doctors. Her parents had thrown her older sister out of the house when she became pregnant. Gina was afraid to tell her parents about the pregnancy itself. To speak of an abortion was unthinkable.

After Gina finally collapsed it was too late. None of her friends were able to attend Gina's funeral, and her parents made sure no one really knew why she died.

But I knew, and I will never forget my lovely, witty, wonderful friend, Gina. She would be here today if abortions had been legal in 1969. How can anyone forget that?

Signed,
Gina's friend

"As a physician, I have a grave, but welcome responsibility to honor and validate my patients when I see them at such vulnerable and psychologically defenseless moments in their lives. I have performed abortions for many tens of thousands of women and I have supported them in their grief and sorrow and have tried to allay some of their universal feelings of shame. Women are to be honored for making these difficult decisions, they do not make them in haste or in a moral vacuum!"

— Suzanne T. Poppema, M.D.
Medical Director
Aurora Medical Services
Seattle, WA

I am deeply concerned about the vague image and perceptions that come to mind when a lot of us think about abortion — and the people who have abortions. As someone who has undergone a legal abortion and someone who has helped a friend obtain an illegal abortion prior to the Supreme Court decision, I would like to share my story in the hope that you will consider the importance of this issue in your lives.

I am your neighbor. I am in my mid-thirties, married, live in a suburb of Seattle and have a full-time position in the investment community. While attending school in another city I helped a fellow student obtain an illegal abortion in an affluent section of the city. The person performing the abortion charged $500, provided no anesthesia or antibiotics, and had a waiting room full of women. She performed ten abortions that evening while my friend and I waited her turn. The feelings and fears in that room still live in my mind. I saw women who against incredible obstacles were undergoing a procedure which made them criminals; women who endured a great deal of physical pain and potential injury, and women like my friend who spent everything they had, plus what their friends could raise, to have an abortion. I shudder to think what happened to the women who didn't have $500 in 1966 ... The one thing these women had in common was their decision to have an abortion — their choice.

In 1970 I became pregnant through failure of my birth control method. The man with whom I had conceived offered to marry me. It was an option I didn't feel I had — there was no way that such a marriage would have worked out, and I knew that my responsibility now extended beyond just myself. I was not financially or emotionally capable of providing a child with the kind of life it deserved, and I could not in good conscience bring such a child into the world. I sought advice from my doctor and the counsel of my minister. I then made my decision — a decision that was right for me then, and one I would repeat given the same

133

set of circumstances. The difference between my abortion and my friend's was that mine was legal, in a hospital and cost $120. The decision to have an abortion was the same for both my friend and myself, only my abortion was obtained legally — my health and life not endangered by someone else's law.

When I was seventeen, I was raped by my father. It was a brutal attack. It was a brutal attack which also left me pregnant. Imagine the double tragedy of such violence. Imagine being seventeen, pregnant after being raped by your father, alone, isolated, afraid to tell anyone for fear your parents would find out and that, if they did, you would be further humiliated, harassed and abused by your father, or that your mother would herself be in danger of abuse should she take your side. I felt and feared all these things.

I decided that an abortion was one of two alternatives for me. My other alternative was suicide. Fortunately, I found a clinic where I was able to obtain supportive counseling as well as an abortion. Fortunately, when I needed an abortion, that right was secure for all women. If I had been unable to obtain an abortion, if I had been forced to obtain parental consent, I would, most certainly, have killed myself. And at seventeen, pregnant and having just survived being raped by my father, the idea of going into court and telling a judge about my situation would have been inconceivable; it took me 7 years to tell anyone the story, much less a judge.

As difficult as it is for me to write my story, I feel compelled to come forward on behalf of the women of this country who face the misogyny of those today who would legislate our bodies and our lives. I write on behalf of the young women today who face similar situations and I write in debt to the women who fought to protect my life. I have not used my name — not because I am ashamed of having had an abortion, but because, ten years later, my father remains a powerful threat.

Lack of abortion rights would not have forced me to bring the pregnancy to term, nor would it have forced me to communicate with my parents. Rather, it would have forced me to take control of my life in the only way left available — suicide. Anti-choice forces are women-hating and dangerous.

* Reprinted from NARAL's *The Voices of Women* booklet

135

They seek to take control of women's bodies and lives. They victimize, in particular, women who are most in need of compassion — compassion and the chance to regain control of their lives.

Right off, first thing I got to tell you is that I'm not for abortion. But I am for it being legal. Here's why. I'm 16 now but when my family moved to Connecticut from Vermont 4 years ago, something real awful happened to me. I never wrote this down before, and I hope I can do it now because you guys who can change the laws need to know about girls like me.

Like I said I was 12 and guess my periods had been coming for about a year. I was walking home from school about the time detention got out because I was being tutored for math which I have lots of problems with still. I took a shortcut through an empty lot. I guess it had been empty real long because the grass was real high. I didn't hear anybody coming and all of a sudden I was grabbed from behind and somebody blindfolded me and shoved me down. I think there were 4 of them. Three held me and the fourth did it to me. They took turns, more than once each, then they tried to take turns stuffing it in my mouth but I gagged so I started choking. I remember they sounded young, maybe 9th graders. I was in 7th.

When I got home my mom wanted to know why I was crying and my clothes were torn and mussed. I was scared she'd be mad if I told her the truth so I said I fell. She looked like she didn't believe me but didn't say any more. When I didn't get my period for a few months I worried it was because of what happened. I was so scared, you know, I stopped being tutored and found girls to walk with even though I worried I'd get them in trouble too. When I didn't get my period that third month and started feeling weird — sick and hungry at the same time, Mom took me to the doctor. He had me pee in a jar and later that day he told Mom I was 3 months pregnant.

Well sir, since I never even had a boyfriend; you can just picture my Mom's reaction. I finally broke down and told her what happened. She felt real bad and cried and hugged me. She said she had to tell Daddy, but my little brother and sister were not to know. She said "Thank the Lord for insurance money and abortion clinics." She took

me to a clinic where they were real nice and didn't act like I was dirt and all. It didn't hurt much; not as much as when those boys raped me. I don't feel like I killed someone like the right-to-lifers say. I feel like the doctor at the clinic took something bad out of me. I still never had a boyfriend. I don't know if I ever will. Mom and Daddy sent me to a therapist and I still go. But the nightmares will happen sometimes. I keep thinking, what if your guys took away legal abortions and those boys or some other boys did that to me again? What would happen to me? I think about it a lot and in my nightmares whether I'm being raped or it already has happened, and I'm pregnant and there's no more abortions.

Please sir can you make the nightmares stop?

Thank you. *

* Reprinted from NARAL's *The Voices of Women* booklet